JH

Life in the Garden

Life in the Garden

PENELOPE LIVELY

VIKING

VIKING

An imprint of Penguin Random House LLC
375 Hudson Street
New York, New York 10014
penguin.com

Grateful acknowledgment is made for permission to quote from 'The Mower' from *Collected Poems* by Philip Larkin (Faber and Faber, 2003), reprinted by permission of Faber and Faber and Farrar, Straus and Giroux; *Rebecca* by Daphne du Maurier (Virago, 2003), reprinted by permission of Curtis Brown Group Ltd, London, on behalf of The Chichester Partnership. Copyright © The Chichester Partnership, 1938; selected works by Elizabeth Bowen, reproduced by permission of Curtis Brown Ltd, London; *Tom's Midnight Garden* by Philippa Pearce (OUP, 2008), reprinted by permission of Oxford University Press; *The Stone Diaries* by Carol Shields (Fourth Estate, 1994), copyright © Carol Shields, 1994, reprinted by kind permission of the Carol Shields Estate; *Green Thoughts* by Eleanor Perényi (Vintage, 2002), copyright © Eleanor Perényi, reprinted by permission of Penguin Random House; *The Middle Age of Mrs Eliot* by Angus Wilson (Faber and Faber, 2011), copyright © Angus Wilson, 1958, reprinted by permission of Faber and Faber; *Arcadia* by Tom Stoppard, reprinted by permission of Faber and Faber and United Agents; 'Burnt Norton' from *Four Quartets* by T. S. Eliot (Faber and Faber, 2001), reprinted by permission of Faber and Faber and Houghton Mifflin Harcourt Publishing Company; 'Seven Types of Shadow' from *Selected Poems* by U. A. Fanthorpe (Enitharmon Press, 2012), reprinted by kind permission of Enitharmon Press; *One Man and His Dig* by Valentine Low (Simon & Schuster, 2008), copyright © 2008 Valentine Low, reprinted by permission of Simon & Schuster UK Ltd.

First published in Great Britain by Fig Tree, an imprint of Penguin Random House UK

Illustrations by Katie Scott

ISBN 9780525558378 (hardcover)
ISBN 9780525558385 (ebook)

Printed in the United States of America
10 9 8 7 6 5 4 3 2 1

Set in Dante MT Std

To Josephine

Contents

Introduction

Virginia Woolf goes gardening one day in May, which sets me thinking about the curious apposition between gardening as reality and as metaphor. Beatrix Potter's swingeing parable about the superiority of rural values—*The Tale of Johnny Town-Mouse*—invites an inspection of the traditional divide between town and country. Willa Cather's prairie gardens made by the American pioneers remind me that gardening can be about control, the conquest of nature, but that it also defies time. My grandmother's garden, deeply influenced by Gertrude Jekyll, in both landscaping and planting, prompts consideration of the vicissitudes of gardening fashion.

The two central activities in my life—alongside writing—have been reading and gardening. And there has been a sense in which the two have meshed: I always pay attention when a writer conjures up a garden, when gardening becomes an element of fiction. I find myself wondering what is going on here. Is this garden deliberate or merely fortuitous? And it is nearly always deliberate, a garden contrived to serve a narrative purpose, to create atmosphere, to furnish a character.

So this is a book in which fictional gardens act as prompts for a consideration of what gardens and gardening have been for us, over time. Why and how do people garden? Why and how have they gardened?

I shall need to get personal. If you have been a gardener, all references to gardens, plants, gardening activities, strike a chord. Am I interested in that? Have I tried this? So there has to be a strand of memoir wound in with everything else: a life in the garden. From the first suburban plot in which my husband and I carefully rescued and planted out a whole lot of willowherb seedlings because we didn't know what they were, to the few square yards of London that are essential today, and where I can still be rapturous about a new hellebore, or purring over the pot of snowdrops positioned so that I can see it from the window.

I grew up in a garden. Almost literally, because this was a hot, sunny garden in Egypt and much of life was lived out of doors. Our home was one of three houses built outside Cairo in the early twentieth century, a sort of alien enclave amid fields of sugarcane and clover, canals and mud-hut villages. All three had large gardens, and my mother had created ours very much in the spirit of the English garden, with lawns, rose beds, lily ponds, pergola walks, and a necessary nod to the climate and what would grow there by way of poinsettias, lantana, zinnias, cineraria and bougainvillea. Though she did once plant daffodil bulbs, which were rightly aghast at what was required of them, and sent up just a few spindly blooms. But, for me, the garden was a kind of intimate paradise, intensely personal, with private hiding places—a twiggy hammock in a hedge where I went to read *Swallows and Amazons* and *Tales from Troy and Greece*, a particular eucalyptus tree with which I was in animistic communion, the bamboo-shaded water garden where tadpoles massed around the roots of the arum lilies. I can still draw a map of this garden in every detail. It no longer exists; the whole of that area has long since been subsumed into Cairo's urban sprawl, but when I went there thirty years ago I felt that its memory must lurk, beneath the slum houses and the rubble, a memory of trees and grass and flowers, and the ghost of my own *alter ego*.

Gardening is genetic, as far as I am concerned, and runs down the female line. In my family, it started with my grandmother Beatrice Reckitt, who made a magnificent garden from the *tabula rasa* of a sloping Somerset field, complete with Gertrude Jekyll-style rill and sunken rose garden, lawns and ha-ha, kitchen garden, summerhouse and potting shed—all the attributes of the serious garden. Her daughter, Vera, my mother, gardened an English garden in Egypt. I graduated from the suburban plot to two successive Oxfordshire gardens, one with two streams running through it. My daughter, Josephine, gardens in a more informed way than any of us; a working musician, an oboist, she took Royal Horticultural Society courses many years ago in spare time that she did not have, and now gardens in London and in Somerset with expertise that I admire and envy. And her daughter Rachel, another musician, seems next in line: a serious engagement with sweet peas last year looked significant.

You don't discover your own gardening potential until you have gardenable space of your own, if only a humble window box. Jack and I were fired up by the suburban plot. Though there might have been a streak of genetic compulsion for him as well: his father had gardened with a sort of fanaticism in the family's council-house garden in Newcastle. A garden in which all expense was avoided, the patch of lawn made from clumps of grass dug up by the roadside, everything grown from seed, seed collected always for next year, runner beans rubbing shoulders with hollyhocks, lettuces nudging alyssum and lobelia. The other end of the spectrum from my grandmother's Somerset acreage, but the drive and the commitment the same. The urge to garden transcends social circumstance, which accounts for the allotment movement, of which more later, and the floral energy of small front gardens up and down the land. I remember a visiting American friend gazing in wonder at the flamboyance of June: "Everyone in this country grows a rose." If three acres and a cow was the land-reform slogan of the nineteenth century, today's requirement would be that minimal plot where a person can grow something, anything, can get their hands into the earth and defy time.

We garden for tomorrow, and thereafter. We garden in expectation, and that is why it is so invigorating. Gardening, you are no longer stuck in the here and now; you think backward, and forward, you think of how this or that performed last year, you work out your hopes and plans for the next. And, for me, there is this abiding astonishment at the fury for growth, at the tenacity of plant life, at the unstoppable dictation of the seasons. As I write, in late winter, the first snowdrops have nosed out of the earth, the ground-cover roses have tiny red knobs that say they are remembering what they have to do come June, a single white choisya flower is unseasonal but obedient—the days are a bit warmer, time to get going. Everything will happen anyway, that is what it is programmed to do, but the point of being a gardener is that you can manipulate this marvelous process, contrive, direct.

But plenty will resist direction, of course. The weeds will fight back. Anthropomorphism is unavoidable, I am finding, in writing about gardening: weeds don't just grow, they grow with intent, they grow aggressively. Well, they do, as any gardener knows. They sneak in and swarm up when your back is turned. There is always this sense that the garden is a living entity, with its own agenda—hundreds of conflicting agendas—and that you are in control only up to a point, a precarious relationship in which it is not clear who has the upper hand. Fanciful, I dare say, and perhaps this animistic view is just the lingering effect of my childhood immersion in *Alice's Adventures in Wonderland* and *Through the Looking-Glass*: "We *can* talk," says the Tiger-lily, "when there's anyone worth talking to." The flowers make personal remarks about Alice (as adults tend to do of children). "You're the right color, and that goes a long way." "You're beginning to fade, you know—and then one can't help one's petals getting a little untidy."

The literary garden may have acted as prompt very early on, for me, reading probably in that personal space within an Egyptian hedge, and reading with that unique, never to be recovered, immersion of childhood reading, when a fictional world invades the real one, and you no longer know quite which is which. I know I talked to that eucalyptus tree when I was a child, and quite possibly to flowers too, wandering from the pages of *Alice* out into the garden.

I don't now, but perhaps I should. Prince Charles does, it seems. In 1986, he was quoted as saying that he spoke to his trees and plants, that it was important to engage with them, and that they responded—though he does not seem to have specified in quite what way. He was ridiculed for this, in some quarters, but somewhat later, in 2009, the Royal Horticultural Society, it was reported, decided to test his theory by reading works of literature to tomato plants by means of attaching the headphones of an MP3 player to their roots. Passages from Shakespeare and from John Wyndham's *The Day of the Triffids* were selected as test recordings, with plant growth to be measured against that of a set of control plants left in silence. Please note that the original newspaper reports of this were dated March 31, 2009, and one could draw the obvious conclusion, were it not that in June of that year the *Telegraph* reported the results; apparently there had indeed been a response from the plants, with read-to plants putting on more growth than those left in silence, and the female voice having an appreciably greater effect. Well, well. I can absolutely see why *The Day of the Triffids* was chosen, but the report does not state if that proved more effective than Shakespeare. If it did, I think we should start to worry.

So much for the sentient plant. What cannot be disputed is that gardens themselves are eloquent, in that they speak for their owners. By their gardens ye shall know them. Back in my days of the Oxfordshire garden with two streams, we used to open up to the public on one day a year, under the Yellow Book listing, the gardens open in aid of charity under the National Garden Scheme. We were part of a village garden opening— four or five of the village gardens being judged worth a visit, I seem to remember. The Yellow Book openings are in aid of charity, and back then there was keen competition between Oxfordshire and Kent to be the county raising the most money. Kent had pipped Oxfordshire to the post the year before, so there was now ferocious endeavor. A Yellow Book person inspects gardens to see if they are up to Yellow Book standards; ours only just crept in, I suspect—it was described as an "Informal cottage-type garden," which is Yellow Book speak for "a bit unkempt and weedy." Nevertheless hundreds of people trooped through, always impeccably mannered, never dropping a cigarette end or a sweetie paper. And it was then that I got talking to a Dutch couple who told me that they came to this country every year specifically to do a tour of Yellow Book openings. I assumed they were keen gardeners themselves. Well, only up to a point, they said; the real value of the tour, for them, was that it gave them such insight into how the English live, the variety of social circumstance, the range of taste and style. I knew exactly what they meant; we too were addicted to Yellow Book visiting, and I remember once finding the National Collection of auriculas in a council-house garden.

We beat Kent that year.

There was an element here of competitive gardening, I suppose. But it was a worthy kind of competition in that it was all about which county gardened to such effect that it raised most money for charity. Gardeners are not by nature competitive, I think; it is more a question of mutual respect which can spill over into emulation. Half the point of garden visiting, Yellow Book or otherwise, is that you can come back with stolen ideas. In the Oxfordshire garden days, we frequently visited Hidcote, one of the National Trust's flagship gardens, and it was the planting of the water garden there that gave me ideas of what could be done with our two streams. Ours were a mere trickle compared with Hidcote's luxuriant stream garden, but never mind—primulas, ferns. Though we made the mistake of putting in some mimulus, the monkey flower, a yellow thug that we then spent years trying to weed out. Hidcote had known better, or had more room.

The area where gardening does get competitive is the flower show, from small-time village effort to the big events. There is admittedly a fascination about scanning the displays: collection of onions exceeding 250g each, three runner beans, heaviest marrow. But who wants a football onion, a yard of runner bean, a marrow like a truncheon? There is a distressing culture at work here: size matters. I'm not very happy either with competing pansies, chrysanthemums and dahlias—they sit there looking stiff and uncomfortable.

The apex of horticultural competition is of course the Chelsea Flower Show. Competition on every front: Best Show Garden, Best City Garden, Plant of the Year, medals Gold, Silver-Gilt, Silver. Gardens get medals, stands get medals, anything gets a medal. Most of the competition is commercial—nurseries vying with one another, professional garden designers fighting it out. Modest satisfaction for the Golds, brave smile if it's a Silver-Gilt, slink off home if it's Silver. I suppose this jacks up tension, but I suspect that the average Chelsea visitor doesn't much care about who got what, they just want to gaze at lots of gorgeous plants and maybe get some tips for their own gardening. On the occasions that I went I used to enjoy overheard comments: "We had one of those, but of course your father killed it." The people could be as interesting as the exhibits. I am not robust enough to do Chelsea nowadays—too much walking and standing. But Jack and I went several times, way back, and for me it was always a question of prizing him away from the lawnmower displays. What is it with men and lawnmowers? Here was an academic, a political theorist, whose mind should have been on higher things, lustfully scrutinizing Mountfields, Hayters, Atcos.

Philip Larkin felt differently. A few years ago the British Library had a sumptuous exhibition called *The Writer in the Garden*. A central exhibit was Philip Larkin's lawnmower, hung on a vertical panel so that you could inspect it closely: a Qualcast. But he did not give it a good press in a letter written after he had bought a 1950s house with a long garden, and was appalled at the idea of having to look after this: "It has a huge garden—not a lovely wilderness (though it soon will be)—a long strip between wire fences—Oh God, Oh God—I am taking on the vendors' Qualcast (sounds like a character in Henry James) . . . I don't know when I shall get in . . . I hope before the bloody garden starts growing . . ."

But the Qualcast was to become an instrument of tragedy. Larkin got to grips with it, and then one day inadvertently killed a hedgehog with it. A poem sprang from that event.

> The mower stalled, twice; kneeling, I found
> A hedgehog jammed up against the blades,
> Killed. It had been in the long grass.
>
> I had seen it before, and even fed it, once.
> Now I had mauled its unobtrusive world
> Unmendably. Burial was no help:
>
> Next morning I got up and it did not.
> The first day after a death, the new absence
> Is always the same; we should be more careful
>
> Of each other, we should be kind
> While there is still time.

Andrew Motion, Larkin's biographer, sees this poem serving as an elegy for the poet's mother. No doubt it does, but it is also about a hedgehog, and is perhaps unique as a poem about a lawnmower.

So far as I am concerned the difference between men and women is that men are interested in cutting grass and women are not. I actually prefer a daisy-sprinkled lawn; Jack, of course, wanted meticulous stripes, and many happy hours were spent achieving these. Marital gardening is a whole subject of its own. The Nicolsons, at Sissinghurst, look like a rather efficient team, with Harold working on the hard landscaping, as we now call it, and Vita on the planting. Beth Chatto was crucially supported by her husband, Andrew, who researched the plants suitable for her plans, while Margery Fish seems to have been both impeded and frustrated by her husband's somewhat conflicting gardening tastes. The rest of us, gardening more humbly, will be familiar with the areas of potential disagreement when gardening in tandem—division of labor, resolution of likes and dislikes. Jack and I gardened pretty harmoniously, on the whole, sharing tastes and aversions. Perhaps unusually, I did much of the vegetable gardening—he rapidly got bored with trenching for potatoes, and I rather enjoyed a good dig.

I remember with envy. A chronic back problem means that digging has been long since out of the question; I can't bend at all now, so my gardening of the London garden has to be restricted to watering, dead-heading, and such operations as I can manage from a folding seat. Help is needed for anything else, and a garden firm once a year to deal with rampant ivy and to high-pressure the paving. This is old-age gardening, and like all other aspects of old age, it creeps up on you, and has to be faced down and dealt with. Some of you will know about this, and empathize, familiar with the strategies and the frustration. My friend Elizabeth Jane Howard was a committed gardener. She too suffered from arthritis, and gardened through it: "It hurts like hell but I do it anyway," she would say. As well as a more formal garden area by her Suffolk home, she had a river-island wild garden, a paradise of trees, bamboo, willows, water lily pond, rambling paths fringed with bluebells. And gardens crept into her novels, of course. I used to spend a weekend with her there from time to time, and enjoy garden talk and the ritual tour of the island.

Nowadays, all my garden talk is with Josephine, who has created, over the last twenty years, a garden for the Somerset cottage that is our toehold there, just down the lane from my grandmother's house and garden, a cottage built by my grandfather in 1929 as the gardener's cottage in the days when you could acquire a bit of land and run up a building if you felt like it. Today, and long since, all that area is part of Exmoor National Park, and you can't lay a finger on a cowshed, let alone propose anything as intrusive as a building. The garden that Josephine has made has areas segueing into one another, defined by yew hedges that are now full height and have been for several years—I had no idea you could establish a yew hedge so quickly. The main borders are by the house, and surround a lawn with a sundial from the old garden in the middle, which leads on to a further yew-enclosed lawn that works nicely for croquet now, and then on through a yew arch into the little orchard, with compost bins and rubbish heap tucked away at the end, beyond beech hedging. The two cherries she planted at the very start to give height to the garden—*Prunus avium*, the native cherry—are mature now, out in full bridal glory in May. Shirley poppies and aquilegia seed themselves, the originals brought from my grandmother's garden, and there are colored primroses from there too, along with the regular primrose. But my grandmother would be surprised by the planting of much of this twenty-first-century garden—*Verbena bonariensis*, hellebores, penstemons, alchemilla, plants not common in her day, and she would have loved them.

But *Erigeron karvinskianus*, the Mexican daisy, would be entirely familiar; it showered down the drystone walls of her rose garden, a Gertrude Jekyll favorite. And, for me, it has become a kind of signature plant; in London, it has obligingly seeded itself all round the railings at the front of my house, and down the iron steps to the basement. And it has spread along this side of the square, colonizing other frontages, where others have clearly welcomed it—only one insensitive neighbor has torched it with weed-killer.

Thus one garden leaves its legacy in another—the butterscotch primroses and the blowsy poppies in Josephine's garden remembering her great-grandmother's. And Josephine's daughter Rachel's small London garden will be stocked almost entirely with plants and divisions from Somerset—the garden center won't get a look-in.

Ah, garden centers. Unavailable, of course, to my grandmother, who had to rely on postal ordering from nurseries. Today, the garden center is a major shopping opportunity. They have a lot to answer for, and I am their ideal customer—

a complete pushover, liable to load up a trolley with anything that catches my eye. They are craftily familiar with the likes of me; they know how to display, how to tempt. The garden center has much to do with gardening fashion—many of us garden according to how the garden center has decided that we should garden, by stocking up with this or that. I am partial to heuchera, as pot plants, and the garden center has led me on, I know, by always having an inviting heuchera selection, set out to best advantage. And the garden center will itself have been steered by whatever is being extolled on television; *Gardeners' World* also determines how the nation is to garden. It was ever thus—there were directing influences for the Victorian and the early-twentieth-century gardener also, of course, as we shall see. But not on such a scale. Garden supply is big business now, reflecting the way in which those who garden have become younger; gardening is no longer a marginalized activity, performed mainly by the middle-aged. A shabby garden is as demeaning as a shabby house, and gardening is no longer seen by younger people as a naff, elderly thing to be doing.

I see gardening as a unifying, bonding experience, despite the competing onions and marrows at flower shows. Neighborly gardening usually involves exchange of cuttings or divisions. Sometimes you can see, looking at a line of front gardens, where someone's flourishing pink or Michaelmas daisy has made its way along the street, handed on to go forth and multiply. Or garden begets garden, as in my family, where descendants of my grandmother's aquilegias and primroses fetch up in her great-great-granddaughter's rather smaller plot.

In a particular part of north London, many gardens have a loquat—yellow fruit and strongly sweet-smelling white flowers—particularly dear to Greek Cypriots, apparently, and thus remembering that many lived in that area. In Kentish Town—and elsewhere in London, I'm sure—the line of trees along the ends of back gardens is a legacy of the field boundaries before the houses came. The tenacity, the antiquity, of plant life is something to look at later, but I find particularly telling the way in which their very names are eloquent, speaking across time: the lily travels back through Anglo-Saxon *lilege* to Roman *lilium*, fennel through *fincul* to *feniculum*, fig back to *ficus*. It is the same kind of eloquence as the place-name; places tell you who has been here, these plants tell who has known them, and spoken of them.

And then there is the personal resonance that a plant can have—the Proustian madeleine effect. The smell of crushed eucalyptus leaves takes me back to that Egyptian garden, the four or five great trees that edged the drive. Rosemary—and I am in Palestine, as it then was, on a hill above Jerusalem, in 1941. Actually, you want Proust to have been more specific about that Combray garden; all you learn is that the madeleine evoked "all the flowers in our garden" and that "the whole of Combray and of its surroundings, taking their proper shapes and growing solid, sprang into being, town and gardens alike, from my cup of tea." You would like some naming of names, but never mind—the point is the effect, the resonance, the power of taste and smell, their ability to summon up another time, another place.

It is becoming more and more apparent that gardens and all that is within them are never just themselves: they are allusive, evocative, and that is why they can be such fertile material for a writer. They are indeed real, earthy, prolific places, and we know them as that, we dig them, enjoy them, but they are also wonderfully referential—they are potent, flexible, can become a metaphor. And that is what I should like to get on to first—the various concepts of the garden, and garden metamorphosis.

Reality and Metaphor

On the 31st of May 1920, Virginia Woolf went gardening. Here's what she wrote in her diary: "The first pure joy of the garden . . . weeding all day to finish the beds in a queer sort of enthusiasm which made me say this is happiness. Gladioli standing in troops; the mock orange out. We were out till 9 at night, though the evening was cold. Both stiff and scratched all over today, with chocolate earth in our nails." This is the commentary of a practical, hands-on gardener, a view of the garden wonderfully different from the way in which gardens surface in her novels. But, before considering that, I want to look at where it was that she was gardening, and what that garden was like.

Virginia and Leonard Woolf bought Monk's House, at Rodmell, near Lewes, in July 1919, when she was thirty-seven. It was an old, weather-boarded house, disconcertingly austere by twenty-first-century standards—no electricity or running water, no bathroom, a privy in the garden, and only gradually did the Woolfs overcome these deficiencies. It had three-quarters of an acre of garden, and this, certainly for Leonard, seems to have been the prime attraction. It is clear that he was the gardener-in-chief, with Virginia as an interested accomplice and frequent assistant. There was already a fine orchard (apples, plums, pears, cherries), and as time went on Leonard laid out the hard landscaping—the creation of a garden composed of discrete areas, or rooms, united by brick-paved paths, that is the basis of the garden as it is today, now in the care of the National Trust.

They evidently flung themselves at the garden with immediate enthusiasm. In September 1919 Virginia wrote: "We have been planting tiny grains of seed in the front bed, in the pious or religious belief that they will resurrect next spring as Clarkia, Calceolaria, Campanula, Larkspur and Scabious." A list of annuals—a nice mix except for the calceolaria, which fills me with horror, a nasty bulbous yellow spotty thing which would have offended the palette of otherwise pinks and blues. I do hope it failed to resurrect. But that was evidently, for Leonard, the start of a tradition of growing from seed; later, he had greenhouses.

Caroline Zoob and her husband, Jonathan, were tenants of the National Trust at Monk's House for ten years, and her fine book—*Virginia Woolf's Garden*—is testimony to their talented management of the garden. The brief was to preserve as much as possible of Leonard's original layout and, indeed, some of the Woolf planting preferences. Leonard and Virginia had a taste for strong colors. "Our garden is a perfect variegated chintz: asters, plumasters, zinnias, geums, nasturtiums and so on: all bright, cut from coloured papers, stiff, upstanding as flowers should be," Virginia wrote in a letter. That description has me a bit doubtful, and the sumptuous photographs in Caroline Zoob's book show planting schemes and palettes rather more subtle and in tune with contemporary taste, though, loyally, zinnias were still grown from seed on their watch, one of Leonard's favorites. Hardly seen elsewhere, nowadays, out of fashion, like the red-hot pokers—kniphofia—that he had (and which flare up in *To the Lighthouse*, as we shall see): "... the garden is full of zinnias. The zinnias are full of slugs. L goes out at night with a lantern and collects snails, which I hear him cracking ..." Virginia may have left pest control to him, but she certainly got weeding: "Very soon, in any occupation, one makes a game of it. I mean ... that one gives characters to weeds. The worst is the fine grass which has to be sifted out conscientiously. I like uprooting thick dandelions and groundsel."

They had a gardener, of course. Essential for a garden that size, and more was added later when Leonard bought the adjacent field, though clearly he always weighed in much himself. A serious, substantial garden, and it was of central importance to Virginia, even if it was Leonard who was the driving force. She worked in her own writing lodge in a corner of the orchard, and her diary is full of moments of appreciation: "The great lily in the window had four flowers. They opened in the night"; "Never has the garden been so lovely ... dazzling one's eyes with reds and pinks and purples and mauves"; "a blaze of dahlias." Vegetables and fruits were grown too—peas, strawberries, beans and lettuce by 1921, and the apples were harvested on an industrial scale.

Leonard's gardening style sounds to have been idiosyncratic, *sui generis*, giving license to personal taste and preference—all those hot colors. No hint of the then-current Gertrude Jekyll influence, say. Vita Sackville-West came there often, that doyenne of early-twentieth-century gardening, but there seems no evidence that she and Virginia talked gardens much, if at all. Virginia herself said that the Monk's House garden was "all Leonard's doing," and Caroline Zoob feels that she was neither knowledgeable nor technically skilled. But the essential point, for me, is that she intensely observed gardens and plants, and that she could get down to it with a will, get her hands dirty, attack the dandelions and the groundsel.

On the 24th of March 1941, she wrote in her diary, "L. is doing the rhododendrons." On the 28th, she walked out of the garden, through the gate at the end, and down to the bank of the river Ouse, where she drowned herself.

So, she was a real gardener, Virginia Woolf; she planted, she weeded, she knew the chocolate earth. But now, here she is when the garden becomes a fictional device: "Flower after flower is specked on the depths of green. The petals are harlequins. Stalks rise from the black hollows beneath. The flowers swim like fish made of light upon the dark, green waters. I hold a stalk in my hand. I am the stalk . . ." This is from *The Waves*, and is the thought process of one of the six characters whose voices tell the story, turn by turn. Louis is a child in this opening section; the other five respond similarly to what they are seeing of the world around them. I can appreciate this as representing the immediacy of a child's vision, but this is merely establishing the tone for the rest of the narrative. Stream of consciousness, of course, and in its most exaggerated form. The garden, in that passage, becomes a vehicle for method, style. There is little narrative in the novel, as such—the six friends grow up, remain connected, meet again all together in later life in two set-piece scenes, react to and discuss a seventh, who is not given a voice. They do emerge as separate personalities—three men, three women—though Virginia Woolf herself said that she meant them in a sense to be not so much separate characters as facets of a single consciousness, and called the book a prose-poem. *The Waves* is remarkable, unique, but I can't enjoy it: too stylized, too exaggerated.

I am much happier with *To the Lighthouse.* We are in stream-of-consciousness territory here again, but more in the sense of individual interior monologues, and a garden surfaces time and again as essential backdrop. This is the novel in which Virginia Woolf exorcized, as it were, the power over her of her long-dead parents. They become father and mother of the eight Ramsay children, in the novel, holidaying in what would now be called their second home, on Skye, in the Hebrides, and later returning there as adults after Mrs. Ramsay's death. In this last section, the garden speaks for time passing, for the long neglect of the unvisited place: "Poppies sowed themselves among the dahlias; the lawn waved with long grass; giant artichokes towered among roses; a fringed carnation flowered among the cabbages . . ." There is precision here: that fringed carnation, which one can visualize, perhaps a pink, or Sweet William, plenty of all three are fringed. And I particularly like the artichokes among the roses. Here is a garden run riot, no longer under control, and making a narrative point.

Elsewhere in the novel, earlier on, there is mention of big clumps of red-hot pokers—kniphofia, not much favored today, and so placing the garden in time, in the early twentieth century—of pampas grass (ditto), of urns of trailing red geraniums, of Mrs. Ramsay wondering whether to send bulbs for planting when she goes home, but if she did, would the gardener remember to plant them? There is reference to the "jacmanna," which is bright violet, and would have had me baffled were it not for a scholarly note in my edition of the book explaining that what is meant is probably *Clematis* "Jackmanii." Oh, I see. How odd, though, that she calls it that; is it a mistaken rendering of the name, or some nickname of the day for this most common kind of clematis? But I love all this detail; it is the garden observed and remembered by a writer who has noticed gardens and plants, could name names, had experienced the chocolate earth herself. It is an aspect of the accuracy that makes *To the Lighthouse* such a vivid, evocative read; a place, a time, a group of people, conjured up through different eyes, differing sensibilities.

And then there is "Kew Gardens," that short story—if you can call it that—which is, I suppose, the essence of modernist writing, and in which, indeed, plants, a garden, are essential features: "From the oval-shaped flower-bed there rose perhaps a hundred stalks spreading into heart-shaped or tongue-shaped leaves half way up and unfurling at the tip red, blue or yellow petals marked with spots of color raised upon the surface; and from the red, blue or yellow gloom of the throat emerged a straight bar, rough with gold dust and slightly clubbed at the end. The petals were voluminous enough to be stirred by the summer breeze, and when they moved, the red, blue and yellow lights passed one over the other, staining an inch of the brown earth beneath with a spot of the most intricate colour." Thus, and more, runs the account of the flower bed, past which walk, in turn, four couples—a husband and wife, an old and a younger man, two women, a courting couple. The detached narrative shifts from the flower bed to the couples, each of whom are shown in a brief exchange which suggests that there is not much communication between them.

They seem to be drifting purposelessly; within the flower bed a snail is also on the move, and the element of the story that I find satisfying is the bold attempt at the point of view of a snail: "Brown cliffs with deep green lakes in the hollows, flat, blade-like trees that waved from root to tip, round boulders of grey stone, vast crumpled surfaces of a thin crackling texture—all these objects lay across the snail's progress between one stalk and another to his goal . . . The snail had now considered every possible method of reaching his goal without going round the dead leaf or climbing over it. Let alone the effort needed for climbing a leaf, he was doubtful whether the thin texture which vibrated with such an alarming crackle when touched even by the tip of his horns would bear his weight; and this determined him finally to creep beneath it." The snail has purpose, a goal, though we never learn what that is; the four couples appear aimless. And for the closing paragraph things dissolve into an impressionist haze: "Yellow and black, pink and snow white, shapes of all these colours, men, women, and children were spotted for a second upon the horizon . . . dissolving like drops of water in the yellow and green atmosphere." This is Virginia Woolf at her most extreme; you either relish it or shy away. The relevance here is that opening account of the flowers, which is both precise and, for me, disturbing, unsettling. What are they? Heart-shaped or tongue-shaped leaves, red, blue or yellow petals with a throat from which emerges a straight bar, rough with gold dust and slightly clubbed at the end. Exact enough—one should be able to identify them, but I am defeated. I have no idea what they are.

A garden, and gardening as an activity, were as earthily real to Virginia Woolf as to anyone else; but in her fiction, gardens and plants are manipulated, reinvented, bent to the purpose of the narrative in question. This happens time and again, as we shall see, in different hands; the fictional garden will have roots in its creator's own experience, but on the page it becomes a metaphor.

And it was ever thus. The garden as image. The primordial garden, first of all. The Garden of Eden seems now a fragmented mythology embracing nudity, snakes, apples, innocence and expulsion, with the garden element somewhere in the background, an image that obtains in most actual representations from the Middle Ages onward. Few pay much attention to what grew there: grass, greenery, perhaps a water feature. The painted Garden of Eden is, invariably, teeming with wildlife. Animals, animals, with Adam and Eve perched in their midst. Cattle, deer, horses, lions alongside a rabbit, and what looks like a unicorn, for Cranach. Tiger, leopard, peacocks, more rabbits, for Brueghel and Rubens. No identifiable flowers or trees. As for Hieronymus Bosch . . .

Back in the days of the Oxfordshire garden with streams, we would take a drink out there in the early evening, and

Jack would say, settling comfortably into one of our sitting places: "Ah, the garden of earthly delights." I don't think he can have had in mind Hieronymus Bosch's painting of that title, which is a grotesque perversion of a garden, a kind of medieval science fiction. It is a triptych; the left-hand panel gives Adam and Eve center stage, Adam sitting on the grass gazing at God, who holds Eve by the hand; in the background, a water feature with Gaudi-esque fountain, and fairly normal-looking elephant, giraffe and other creatures. It is in the large central panel that the sixteenth-century imagination gets into its stride. Innumerable nude figures are apparently behaving badly against a backdrop of, yes, turf, hedges, more water features and exotic ornaments, but that is all that is garden-like. The figures are mainly androgynous, with the occasional breasts or hint of a penis, and are shown upside down in a pond, inside a giant mussel shell, mounted on a procession of animals which are both realistic and fantastical, carrying a monster strawberry, and in fact generally conforming to some mysterious surreal aesthetic agenda. Scholarly opinion is divided, it seems, as to whether the work serves as a warning about moral decadence, or some celebration of a lost paradise. Maybe that's the "garden" reference. Though, if an image of the Garden of Eden, it does indeed give pause for thought; even the most committed naturist would be inclined to steer clear of this scene.

Paradise Lost is the prime textual account of the nature of the original garden. Milton has Satan as the witness, and he seems to be describing an extensive place; there are groves, lawns, level downs, grots and caves, a lake, a fountain. The furnishings are quite specific in some areas: nectarines, golden apples, purple grapes, along with roses (thornless roses, at that), acanthus, laurel and myrtle, iris, jasmine, violet, crocus, hyacinth, "flowers of all hue." "All beasts of the earth" too, with lions, bears, tigers named, and leopard, lynx, elephant and, of course, the ominous serpent. And since Satan takes the form of a toad in order to whisper corruption into the ear of sleeping Eve, we must assume he got the idea from toad presence. Birds are noted collectively only, except for the nightingale. The place evoked does indeed sound paradisiacal, while the animals appear stripped of ferocity, merely gamboling, the lion dandling a kid. And Adam and Eve are the ancestral gardeners: "their sweet gardening labour."

Efforts have been made, over time, to identify the location of the Garden of Eden. There is a Mesopotamian myth of a king, as primordial man, who was placed in a garden to guard the tree of life. Genesis says that God had planted a garden toward the east, in Eden, causing to grow there "every tree that is pleasing to the sight and good for food." Rivers are named, including the Euphrates. Popular speculation has thus favored southern Mesopotamia—present-day Iraq. The Mormons, on the other hand, insisted that the garden was in Missouri.

There is no mention of vegetation, apart from these trees, but an abundance of animal life must be presumed, since God had already set about mass creation, and Adam had subsequently been invited to name everything: "And God made the beast of the earth after his kind, and cattle after their kind, and everything that creepeth upon the earth . . ."

We gardeners may wish that He could have held back when it came to vine weevil and greenfly.

I suppose literal interpretations of the Bible need to identify a site, to be true to their own logic, but the account of the garden does seem so self-evidently a myth, an image. Nevertheless, the need for a real, findable, garden has persisted in some quarters. Matthew Kneale's superb novel *English Passengers* makes use of the belief held by some actual nineteenth-century fantasist that the garden was sited in Tasmania. In the novel, a clergyman, fanatical in this belief, is one of a trio of Victorian gentlemen who succeed in more or less hijacking a ship crewed by Manxmen and sail to Tasmania where, eventually, they plunge into the bush in search of the site, accompanied by a young Aborigine. The book vividly depicts Tasmanian society of the day, with its greed, brutality, and the rounding-up of the Aborigines, which makes nicely ironic the placing of the Garden of Eden at the site of the most comprehensive ethnic cleansing operation ever. Unless, of course, you count the expulsion of Adam and Eve as such.

For those of us who prefer to take our Garden of Eden as a pungent myth, sited nowhere but within a cosmic imagination, there is the telling parallel meaning: paradise. The garden was paradisiacal, a paradise lost. The etymology here is intriguing, linking indeed the two concepts of a garden and of paradise. The word "garden" descends from an ancient Indo-European word for an enclosure; "yard" and "orchard" derive from the same roots—and Americans call a garden a yard, so, an entirely prosaic and practical meaning. But the word "paradise" is also of old Middle Eastern origin—Iranian—meaning an enclosure, again, but more particularly, walled estates or royal parks. Prosaic and practical once more, but the two seem closely related, and have mutated over time into the dual concept of paradise as a possible afterworld for the virtuous, and as an especially delectable earthly place. The term "paradise" gets flung around at will. Google's initial entry places it in Kensal Green (late-night parties at a bohemian, vintage-styled pub restaurant—I get the idea). And of course Cornwall has its own Eden project, with vast biomes housing rainforests and more.

So the concept of the garden carries overtones of paradisiacal potential. We may not feel that in our own, on a wet day with the weeds rampant, and the slugs and the snails and everything that creepeth upon the earth, but it is instructive to bear in mind the age-old implications of the terminology, of garden ancestry.

Both the practice of gardening and the idea of the garden mutate over time. If the concept springs from Eden itself, the practice seems to have been around far back into antiquity. There is both imagery and archaeological evidence for ancient Egyptian gardening. A tomb painting from around 1500 B.C. shows a pharaoh and his wife inspecting a rather formal-looking garden with date palms, sycamores (a kind of fig—nothing to do with our sycamore) and a water feature that, apart from the lotus and papyrus, would look quite comfortable as a show garden at Chelsea. Excavations have found evidence of the remains of gardens—flower beds, planting pits for trees that were supplied with water from irrigation ditches. At Amarna, wells and artificial lakes have been identified. Gardening would have been a struggle, in that dry climate, and therefore a luxury for the rich and powerful. I am reminded of the endless watering that went on in the Egyptian garden of my childhood—hoses hauled hither and thither, and, once a month, the event known as the flood, when the gardeners were allowed to make a temporary breach in the ditch that was fed from a nearby canal, letting water flow all over the garden for a few hours. Lovely—little fish swimming in the rose beds.

The Hanging Gardens of Babylon appear to be as elusive as the Garden of Eden when it comes to a definitive siting—the only one of the seven wonders of the ancient world that has not been located. There is plenty of archaeological evidence for Babylon itself, of course, about fifty miles south of Baghdad, but apparently no hint of the gardens, which, as described by classical writers, were a massive structure, built by King Nebuchadnezzar in about 600 B.C. Tier upon tier of terraces were planted with mature trees, so that the whole appeared like a tree-covered hillside in this barren landscape. I get interested once more in the watering problem; machines raising water from the river are mentioned, a screw mechanism, Archimedes' Screw. And the Egypt of my childhood again waves a hand—a form of Archimedes' Screw was used there then, a familiar sight in the fields around our home, this large tube-screw being churned by a fellah in order to raise water from one level to another. *Plus ça change* . . . But there is much argument, it seems, about the Hanging Gardens, and whether, if they existed at all, they may not in fact have been at Nineveh, also in Iraq, at the site of present-day Mosul, where the Assyrian king Sennacherib had his palace, and, according to some scholars, has greater claims to have been the ultimate garden designer. The descriptions of the gardens all have them made of courses of mud bricks, and it is easy to imagine that such a construction would have been entirely likely to collapse over time, and moreover that any conceivable archaeological evidence would be hard to interpret. Whoever built it—or nobody, and the whole thing a myth—the idea of a cliff-like garden, these trees up in the air, is wonderfully attractive. And, reality or imagination, the Hanging Gardens seem, alongside the Garden of Eden, to endorse the significance of the garden as a concept. There are real gardens, but we also create gardens in the mind.

Moreover, the notion that a garden may be practical but should have paradisiacal overtones seems to go far back. Those pharaonic gardens clearly had their useful side—all the dates and figs—but were pleasure places for those thus privileged.

We seem to know plenty about Roman gardening practices, and Romans clearly had this dual view of the garden, with the surviving evidence leaning much toward the garden as site of leisure and enjoyment. Those glorious wall frescoes from Pompeii say it all, so evidently painted as a celebration of a garden, harmonies of blue and green with meticulous and entirely identifiable trees and flowers— roses, lilies, daisies. This is art responding to cultivated nature in the same way as Monet at Giverny nearly 2,000 years later. And, in nice confirmation, there is also, at Pompeii, archaeological evidence of those trees and shrubs by way of voids in the subsoil left by their roots, voids which had filled up over time with small pumice pebbles from deposits on top of the soil. These cavities could be cleared and filled with liquid plaster, thus achieving a cast of the roots, which could then be identified. Just as by the same method casts of the bodies of buried Pompeiians could be created.

Pompeiian gardening, like Roman gardens throughout the Roman world, seems to have mainly favored the peristyle garden, the enclosed courtyard garden with planted beds, small trees and shrubs, occasional statuary, perhaps a pool, perhaps box hedging (the Romans had a passion for box, it seems; I wonder if they were plagued by box blight, as today), with shady colonnades all around. I have always thought that the perfect concept of the garden, and have aspired to one—fat chance, in garden moves that have taken me from Swansea to Sussex to Oxfordshire to London. In fact, it is really a design for hot climates, with the house segueing into the garden, and the colonnades for shade; the Frick Gallery in New York has one, delectable, but it has to have glass roofing, so can't be the real thing. In this country, the Roman villa at Fishbourne had a large courtyard with pool and colonnaded cloister-like walkways all around— the same idea but on a much bigger scale, and so lacking the enticing intimacy of the peristyle garden. But this was a proper garden, with lawns, topiary, fountains, box hedging, gravel paths. Labor-intensive to a degree; there must have been a small army of slaves picking weeds out of the gravel, clipping the box, scything the grass. And Roman gardening implements are apparently the ancestors of our own: spades, rakes, hoes, shears, sickles, pruning knives—demonstrating that if a design is initially efficient, you can't improve on it.

This was luxury gardening, for the wealthy and powerful, but there is plenty of evidence that for most Romans utilitarian gardening was combined with the pleasure garden—kitchen gardens at the back of a villa, planted with fruit trees and vegetables, and already establishing the concept of the garden as providing gratification on two fronts: it should delight the senses, and you could also eat it. And it seems that in this country the Romans had a hand in our own garden landscape: they introduced much of what we grow today—walnuts and figs, the sweet chestnut, plums, mulberries, the quince. And—with the Latin derivation of names a giveaway—lily, rose and violet. That is why those painted gardens of Pompeii look so familiar. Though it seems the Romans also introduced ground elder, as a cure for gout, which is unfortunate.

There were around 1,000 Roman villas in Britain by the end of the Roman period. It is easy to imagine them in subsequent abandonment, doing what a neglected garden does, subsiding under nettles and brambles, perhaps plowed up in later centuries, but leaving here and there those indelible traces for some archaeologist to discover and interpret. Gardens are tenacious, reluctant to vanish entirely; they leave some hint of their existence—planting holes, the suggestion of a flower bed or a path.

When I was very young I used to poke around in second-hand bookshops, occasionally finding something I could afford. What a deprivation, today, the loss of those ubiquitous high-street bookshops—you can't poke around like that in Abe Books or Used Book Search. I thus acquired a modern edition (1932, the original is of course 1653) of Culpeper's *Complete Herbal*. I can't think why—this was long before my gardening days, but I know I was fascinated by the line drawings and the confident, archaic texts. I have the book today: "Anemone (Anemone Pulsatilla). The leaves provoke the terms mightily, being boiled and the decoction drunk. The body being bathed with the decoction of them cures the leprosy. The leaves being stamped and the juice snuffed up the nose, purgeth the head mightily." And it is a good read still, robustly instructive; there is nothing that can't be dealt with by a herb—cancers, colic, the sciatica, ague, jaundice, gnawings of the stomach, gravel in the kidneys, proceedings of wind. All you needed to do was get out there and collect the right plant. But it is all very well making light of it; in the age of antibiotics and the NHS, it is hard to imagine what home doctoring must have been like. And the need explains the essential presence of the herb garden, throughout the Middle Ages, and before, and after.

I was obsessed with landscape history, at one time, fired up by the great W. G. Hoskins and other historians of landscape, and I used to prowl over the Oxfordshire countryside in search of ridge and furrow, drove roads. I found the concept of the deserted medieval village particularly arresting; there was one not far away, Hampton Gay, where you see the lumps and bumps where village houses had been, the depressions of the fish ponds. It was the thought of all that lost and distant domesticity that was so striking, the memory of small crofts and their owners preserved there in the twentieth-century grassland. And the crofts had had gardens, so clearly shown on aerial photos. Jenny Uglow, in her masterly *A Little History of British Gardening*, brings such a scene to life: "If we stepped back in time into those narrow lanes . . . we would see thatched cottages with roughly finished walls, each with enclosed ground in front, planted with cabbages, onions, parsley and herbs. The flowers in these gardens were mostly brought in from the fields and carefully cultivated—primroses, cowslip and oxlip, verbascums and mallows." Behind, there would have been the long, rectangular plot, where fruit trees would have grown with vegetables, herbs and flowers. Such medieval peasants were tenant farmers, cultivating the village's open fields but also owing services to the lord of the manor, and these gardens were an essential adjunct to farming in a subsistence economy. But they are also the ancestors of the English cottage garden as we think of it (though hardly know it, now), and as noted and respected in the early twentieth century by Gertrude Jekyll, who admired both the vernacular building materials and the planting styles—pinks, wallflowers, pansies, Sweet Williams hanging over the edges of paved paths.

The cottage garden is in a way ancestral to every modest garden from the medieval period onward. Because after that comes the great divide between patrician gardening—grand gardening—and ordinary, plebeian gardening, with gentry gardening somewhere in between. We tend to know more about patrician gardening, because many great gardens still survive, cherished by the National Trust, more often than not. And features from these seeped down into the aspiring gentry garden: knot gardens, topiary, graveled walks. The Jacobean grand garden favored water—fountains and grottoes—maybe prompting the urge for a water feature that sees many a membrane-lined pond squeezed into the suburban garden of today. But at the lower social level gardening would always have been functional first and foremost: the essential fruit—apples, pears, cherries, blackcurrants, gooseberries, raspberries—all the vegetables, salad leaves for summer, and those vital herbs in all their variety. The edible, salable garden, and then some indulgence where possible—the hollyhocks and marigolds and maybe a rose.

This chasm between the patrician and the plebeian garden persists today. We visit the grand garden, pay dues to the National Trust (probably), admire the vista, the serpentine rill, the cascade, the parterre, the topiary, or the white garden, the stream garden, the laburnum walk (depending on period of garden), and then go home to cast a critical eye over our own inadequate plot. We have probably pinched something—not literally but in terms of an idea, a note about a plant. Could I fit in an arbor with *Clematis tangutica*? Let's get that *Sorbus* "Joseph Rock." Style and content have always filtered down; though, interestingly, in the case of Gertrude Jekyll they filtered up, with her (and Lutyens's) preference for vernacular building materials and cottage-garden plantings. Plenty of that sort of thing to be seen at the Chelsea and Hampton Court show gardens of today—the informal, subtly uncontrived garden with rustic features and jostling growth making the affair of geometric design, arresting materials and feature plantings look brash and artificial. It is a taste that is long-lived, surviving the

Victorian incursion of carpet bedding—blocks of vibrant color, reds, blues, yellows, penned into meticulously shaped beds, a fashion at its last gasp today in some moribund areas of municipal gardening.

Ah, the Victorian garden. Photographs in a hundred-year-old family album show my grandmother's first ever garden, in St. Albans, with circular beds planted each with a standard rose, and bordered with an edging of alyssum and lobelia, planted alternately. She had not yet come across Gertrude Jekyll and William Robinson and was, presumably, remembering what her own mother had done, whose gardening practice would have been rooted firmly in the mid-nineteenth century.

The Victorian garden was all about formality—plants whipped into submission, flowers rated according to color performance. Though, that said, there was more going on in the gardening world, not least a fervent demand for all the new plant arrivals of the time, brought from China and elsewhere by the botanical collectors of the age, of whom more later. And an attention to gardening possibilities from the rising middle class, who were catered for by John Claudius Loudon, the prolific horticultural and landscape design writer, who published, alongside much else, the first, and widely influential, gardening journal *The Gardener's Magazine*, and *The Suburban Garden and Villa Companion*. I like that title—both ponderous and nicely precise. Precise also was his categorization of gardens into four types: those pertaining to grand mansions with over ten acres; establishments with bay windows and gardens of two to ten acres; third-raters around seventeen feet wide with long gardens;

and the fourth-rate terraced house with fourteen-foot front-age and small back garden. You would have known where you were with John Loudon; I know where I am today, as owner of a fourth-rater, in whose small back garden I appreciated the "Tête-à-Tête" daffodils this morning, inspected the new *Hydrangea paniculata* "Limelight" for signs of spring growth, and chivvied out one of those darn foxes. None of these a likely feature of the Victorian garden, except perhaps the fox—but maybe the urban fox is a contemporary addition. Loudon's was class-system gardening, providing advice and information appropriate to the individual reader, according to their gardening status. He was widely popular, and his magazine can be seen as the forerunner of the gardening journals of the early twentieth century, notably William Robinson's *The Garden*, and of today's wealth of commercial garden advice and instruction, and, indeed, of television's influence on the nation's gardening. Though if *Gardeners' World* classifies its viewers, it is discreet enough not to let that show; the program is robustly democratic, serving up suggestions that cater for pretty well everyone, whether you are pruning a solitary rose, or coping with a vegetable garden on a Victorian mansion scale.

Kitchen garden, the Victorians called it, and, forget the carpet bedding, I have a distinct weakness for the Victorian kitchen garden. Those high walls for espalier fruit, the glasshouses, the cold frames, the asparagus beds, the scritch-scratch of Mr. McGregor's hoe . . . But I am getting ahead of myself—Peter Rabbit and Mr. McGregor are for later . . . The Victorian kitchen garden is alluring, satisfying, as a world of its own, dedicated to food production, but in a spacious, elegant,

ritualistic way. Grapes in those glasshouses, a year-round supply of all the basic necessities—the potatoes, the onions, the
carrots and all that, the apples for storing in the apple house.
Labor-intensive, privileged, it is suggestive of a way of life
hard now to envisage. Today, when grapes come from the
supermarket and are nothing to get excited about (and pine-
apples too, another delicacy for the Victorian dining table, and
fiendishly difficult to coax into fruition in a northern greenhouse), the upper class need for show-off table displays seems
just rather bizarre. But behind it was the atavistic drive to
impress: the fancy bowl of fruit showed you had the resources
to grow it, and a head gardener with the skill to do so.

The demise of the Victorian garden is for another chapter.
We have been looking here at the apposition between reality and metaphor, where gardens are concerned, and a run
through the evolution of the garden in reality was relevant.
But there is one further use of the garden in the service of
art that has to be considered: the painted garden.

Monet's water lilies must be an image familiar to many
who have barely heard of the painter, let alone his garden
at Giverny. The palette of blues and greens; that bridge.
Why is it that a photograph of the same scene, however perfectly composed, does not have the same effect, cannot
carry the same weight? I have a stack of hefty books filled
with sumptuous garden photography, and I know that I
like—appreciate—the photos, but I do not look at them
with the same intensity that I look at a painted garden—
painted by a masterly hand. The photograph reports; the
painting examines, interprets, expands.

It has to be the intervention of a different vision. The water lilies are no longer the water lilies that I would see, or that the camera would faithfully reproduce, but have undergone a reincarnation. We see them as Monet saw them, and the effect is startling, illuminating. The water lilies had a potential that was conjured up by other eyes. Eyes—and skill. When it comes to how it is done, I am silenced. You look more closely at the painting; how could he so distribute dots and splashes of paint, contrive certain alignments of color, that the effect would be thus? How could he transfer what the eye saw, and wanted to demonstrate to others, to the hand that held the brush? I don't know. Perhaps you do, if you are a painter and if you have the words for it. For me, it has to remain this mystery.

Claude Monet seems almost the painterly complement to Virginia Woolf in the way that he combined practical, applied gardening with use of the garden as image. He created the garden of his house at Giverny quite deliberately as subject matter: a garden for inspiration and to paint. Indeed, he called it "my most beautiful work of art." And he did so in the most practical, hands-on manner, laying out the long, rectangular beds and square areas or orchards in front of the house when he went there in 1883, later extending the property to create the water garden beyond, which would become the prompt for his greatest works. He made himself into a plantsman, attending the summer exhibition of the French Horticultural Society in 1891 to get ideas for Giverny—tulips, anemones, narcissi, Spanish irises, large-flowered clematis. This was a time of great horticultural activity in France—new botanical introductions from China and elsewhere, hybridization. Monet took an acquisitive interest in new introductions, seeking out in particular hybridized chrysanthemums and water lilies. His chrysanthemums inspired an innovative painting of 1897 in which a mass of pink, red and gold heads are seen flat, without horizon, as though you looked straight at them, like wallpaper, or a carpet, a technique he would develop further in the series known as the *Grandes Décorations*, the great water lily paintings.

As for the water lilies, it seems that new possibilities had been opened up by the crossing of exotic and hardy species to create new, hardy, colored hybrids. And yes, you can see in the water lily paintings, in all their shimmering complexity, that the flowers are pink, red, white, yellow, blue.

Water lilies are of the genus *Nymphaea*—the lovely name inspired by the nymphs of Greek and Roman mythology, and the name Monet gave to his series of water lily paintings when exhibited in Paris—*Nymphéas*. The water lily is one of several genera of plants known as lotuses, and the lotus is of course a frequent motif in ancient Egyptian wall paintings and architecture. The Egyptian water lily is blue, or white, and here I am taken back once more to the garden of my childhood: my mother had made a large pond on which floated white and blue water lilies, with a weeping willow alongside (dear me, pure Monet—is that what she had in mind?). For me, the fascination was the great leaf pads, which often held a pool of water in which trapped tadpoles wriggled around.

A friend took me to Giverny for an eightieth-birthday treat. The modern garden, restored after long years of neglect and opened to the public in 1980, is faithful to Monet's garden in its basic layout, but with the planting no longer the masses of a single color that Monet had designed but a mixed border style with different varieties mingled everywhere—wonderful combinations of color and texture that give an entirely different effect from season to season. Monet had laid out, as well as his main beds and the dramatic Grande Allée, a palette of thirty-eight smaller "paintbox" beds, in parallel rows, trial beds where he could test new introductions for color and habit before massing them together for effect. Again, the practical gardener supplying material for the artist.

Monet was to spend forty years at Giverny, until his death in 1926, but he was there for twelve years before starting to paint the garden. In the initial years of its creation, he did much of the work himself, with his children roped in as a labor force. Later, when success had made him better off, eight gardeners were employed, and by 1900 his response to the garden was such that his painting technique was directed by the garden itself, above all the water garden. It is intriguing to compare early paintings—*Women in the Garden* of 1866—entirely representational, white-clad women with swirling skirts, one with a little pink parasol—and *Lady in the Garden* of 1867—precisely depicted lady in white, again, another parasol, a floriferous standard rose in the middle of a bed of red geraniums, backdrop of dark trees, slice of hard blue sky. You look at these, and it is quite impossible to anticipate the *Grandes Décorations* of the early 1900s—the unique, innovative, self-contained world of watercolors, lilies, reflections. Similarly *The Artist's*

Garden at Vétheuil of 1881, where two children stand staring at the viewer from garden steps that rise vertically through the middle of the painting, with banks of tall yellow-orange flowers on either side. Again, the water lilies to come are from an entirely different vision.

Other Impressionists had gardens, and painted gardens. Bonnard lived within walking distance of Giverny, and cultivated a *jardin sauvage* in contrast to Monet's more contrived effect, influenced perhaps by William Robinson's book *The Wild Garden* of 1870. Caillebotte was also a skilled gardener, but neither of these seems to have had quite Monet's dedication as an applied horticulturalist. He had an impressive library, with specialist books on the cultivation of irises, chrysanthemums, dahlias (three of his favorites), and himself oversaw all the growing from seed, the trial and error. This is what makes the whole Giverny exercise so intriguing—the expert and practical as facilitators, as prompts for artistic experiment and achievement.

The water garden was a later addition to the main garden— the rafts of water lilies, the banks planted with bamboo, flowering cherry, weeping willows, agapanthus, irises. That bridge. The hump-back bridge—delicate, see-through with its slender struts, eventually covered with *Wisteria sinensis*—was inspired by those in the Japanese woodblock prints of Utagawa Hiroshige (Monet owned some). The arch of it—before the wisteria canopy—would provide the bold central sweep in paintings of 1899, as the same scene responded to changing light, the pouring willows reflected between the horizontals of the water lily drifts.

The water lily paintings are the great departure, Monet's

triumphant capture of an environment of water, light and air that changed and changed again, so that several paintings may have the identical subject, but be entirely different. What is at issue now is the nature of art itself, for which the plants, the created landscape, are the prompt, the source of effect after effect of light and color. Monet's creation of Giverny, and his work there, seem a unique instance of art inspired by a deliberately contrived environment.

One artist, one way of using a garden. And there have been others. The Royal Academy's 2016 exhibition *Painting the Modern Garden: Monet to Matisse*, and its accompanying catalog, offered an unparalleled opportunity to consider what a number of painters did with gardens—far from just a collection of agreeable paintings of flowers, but an illuminating demonstration of differing responses to dahlias and chrysanthemums and roses and lilies and grass and trees and the garden path (remarkable how often a path served as compositional feature). For other Impressionists too, the garden was a study of light and color. Manet's *Young Woman among Flowers* is a luminous figure in white against a background of glowing green and yellow, contemplating flowers that are unidentifiable drifts and splodges of blues and pinks. Berthe Morisot's *Woman and Child in a Meadow* has the seated woman playing with her child amid swirling grasses, all color and movement. A meadow, not a garden, but the difference is academic—the point is the atmospheric treatment of nature, of plants.

Everyone painted dahlias—Renoir, Caillebotte, Monet. What was it about the dahlia? Color, I imagine, and contrasting color and texture—the dahlia is wonderfully various. Out of fashion for a while—labor-intensive, can be too assertive—but back in favor now. I remember my grandmother's two large beds above the rose garden: tulips and wallflowers for spring, and then up with those and in with massed dahlias for summer and autumn, the tubers carefully overwintered in the potting shed. Much work; much effect. Late-nineteenth-century France clearly favored the show dahlia bed, never mind the staking and the tuber storing. Renoir painted one—vibrant reds and oranges—as did Monet in *The Artist's Garden in Argenteuil* of 1873, and Renoir painted the young Monet painting that, in a kind of artistic symbiosis; oddly, the two paintings could almost be by the same hand, and I find myself wanting to know if the dahlias are cactus or pompon or those blowsy, full-petaled ones—you can't quite tell, the Impressionist dahlia is a somewhat hazy affair.

Chrysanthemums got them going too, serving up the same color variety and contrast—raided to the full in Monet's 1897 painting that masses them into a single, horizonless display. Caillebotte saw promise in the humble nasturtium, using the same technique in a painting that has red nasturtiums and their gray-green leaves against a pink-mauve background, again like a wallpaper design.

Particular flowers, then, offer possibilities, but the concept, the perception of the garden, was crucially important. This is the use of a garden for the creation of mood and atmosphere, with a place of privacy and tranquility at one end of the spectrum, and much else at the other end. Bonnard's *The Family in the Garden* has a richly textured and colored garden in which a woman and half a dozen or so children are scattered around, playing with a ball, sprawled on the grass. His *Earthly Paradise* goes considerably further. We seem to be back with the

Garden of Eden; a naked man—pink man with blue and red highlights—stands with his back to a tree, gazing into a blue-and-mauve distance, a little apart from the woman reclining on her back, hands behind her head, her body white tinted with blue. A palette of strong colors—blues, greens, dappled with yellow light. No animals in Bonnard's Eden, but the man holds something in his hand. The apple? Paul Gauguin too has an Adam and Eve, the garden barely apparent, just dark foliage as a backdrop to the two dominating orange-ocher figures, the woman with Asian features, the only animals a duck and what seems to be a miniature donkey.

Édouard Vuillard's gardens become disturbing. *Women in the Garden* is all orange, ocher, red and green—two figures against indefinable swirls of color, possible flowers reduced to pink, red or yellow blobs. A diminished, uncomfortable garden. And *Beneath the Trees* displays a garden you really wouldn't want to spend time in—dark and gloomy with three figures at the foot of a tree that is one of the two great white columns of tree trunks that dominate the painting, supporting the dark canopy of leaves, and reducing the human figures to insignificance.

The German Impressionist Max Liebermann had a garden at Wannsee, a suburb of Berlin, which became the subject of 200 of his paintings. It looks like a fairly formal garden, with beds islanded in grass, but if he was dahlia-addicted you wouldn't know—all his flowers are drifts and smudges, though I suspect roses in *Garden Beds with Paths and Flowers*, and yes, he wields a path time and again as compositional device. His trees are delectable, a soft palette of all the greens, but he is not capturing fleeting effects like Monet; rather, he is thought to have been expressing his feelings about nature, and interpreting the timelessness of nature itself.

With Emil Nolde we are moving into Expressionism, and the paintings done of his Danish garden are exuberant with color, rich massed reds, blues, yellows, but plenty of identifiable flowers—purple irises and red roses in *Flower Garden* of 1922, white peonies and orange-purple irises in 1916—an applied gardener, again, with the garden in the service of an exploration of color.

And then there is Matisse. He was another gardener, ordering seeds from catalogs, fascinated by nature: "Flowers provide me with chromatic impressions that remain indelibly printed on my retina . . . So, the day I find myself, palette in hand, in front of a composition, that memory may suddenly spring within me and help me." His garden paintings are interestingly different. In *Tea in the Garden* of 1919 two women sit by a table under trees, a dog scratching itself in the foreground, the garden path (yes, again) leading away up the painting to a lawn beyond, not a flower in sight. Whereas *Young Women in the Garden* (same year) has a girl in white lying on a rug, or possibly a sofa, in the foreground, propped on one elbow and either bored or cold-shouldered by the two others who sit at a table beyond. Again, no flowers. Though in *Acanthus* of 1912, there are robust vivid green acanthus leaves against a cobalt-blue background from which shoots up the purple trunk of a tree—a striking palette of green, blue and mauve.

I think of Gustav Klimt mainly as the creator of all those *fin-de-siècle* golden ladies, but he did indeed paint flowers also. There is his *Cottage Garden* of 1905, an elegant pyramid in which a peak of white chrysanthemums rises from a base of poppies, marguerites, petunias, asters. And two dark crimson dahlias in one corner. No horizon, no background, nothing but a flourish of flowers. He was enjoying, it seems, the traditional German farm garden.

All these are different approaches to the atmospheric garden and, apart from Vuillard's rather disturbing take, celebrate the inspirational possibilities of the garden, as offering a refuge, a personal sanctuary. But, at the other end of the spectrum, the atmospheric garden becomes something else entirely. We may as well start with the most unnerving.

Edvard Munch's *Jealousy in the Garden*, 1929, is apparently one of eleven painted versions of *Jealousy* (including one called *Jealousy in the Bath*). In the foreground is a huge white triangular face with staring brown eyes and down-turned mouth—definitely first cousin to the figure in *The Scream*. At the back, to one side of an angry, dark-trunked central tree (the only identifiable garden element), two people stand together, presumably the objects of jealousy, and to the right is another, solitary figure, perhaps observing, perhaps counseling. What is going on here? The painting clearly has a story to tell, and the garden, as such, is incidental but is nevertheless the setting. In *Apple Tree in the Garden*, Munch has no figures and no story, but his apple tree is again disconcerting, an indigo-blue trunk and a green canopy studded with yellow-green blob apples, a very 1920s-looking house in the background.

Paul Klee, with his *Death in the Garden*, is quite as alarming as Munch. A composition of geometrical shapes, flushed with ocher, green and pink, the only suggestion of a garden being a scatter of stylized trees, each just a few brushstrokes, and left of center an awkwardly sprawled naked woman, possibly pregnant, head lurched to one side against a suggestive pool of red. Oh dear. And when Klee offers *White Blossom in the Garden*, the uneasy flower is made up of four spiky protrusions above a mesh of curving bands of color—yellow, blue and contrasting greens. His picture of a *Garden in Dark Colours* is more satisfying as a painting—wavy color shapes against a deep brown-black background, but you search hard for the garden implications. And, intriguingly, it seems that in fact Klee was fascinated by plants and their structure and many hundreds of his works are based on plant imagery; moreover, he was himself an energetic and skilled gardener.

Van Gogh said that he discovered the laws of simultaneous color contrast while studying flowers. This is the effect of interaction between colors, so that two colors seen together modify each other—red appearing more orange when in proximity to blue, and blue appearing green when in proximity to red. His painting of *Daubigny's Garden in Auvers*, 1890, is all swirl and shape—curved beds with swirling green-brown plants, highlighted in white or pink, and some possible red geraniums, daubs and dashes of white and ocher against green for the grass, an effect of energy, and, yes, intriguing color contrasts, a response to the complexity of nature. But, during the year he spent in the asylum at Saint-Rémy, he painted *Le parc de l'hôpital, à Saint-Rémy*, and himself described it in a letter as an expression of his melancholy: "You'll understand that this combination of red ochre, of green saddened with grey, of black lines that define the outlines, this gives rise a little to the feeling of anxiety." Restless swirls of leaves for the trees, one of which has had a branch lopped off, and appears starkly amputated, the sky overcast with just glimpses of blue at the horizon, a small figure in blue quite dwarfed by the trees, two benches on which nobody sits—no, this is not a comfortable park.

So that is what a selection of artists did with a selection of gardens. And what becomes clear is that in their hands a garden—a flower—is never just a garden or a flower, but a resource for the exploration of color possibilities, of the evanescence of light and movement, the study of form and structure. Or, for the expression of mood and emotion, the capture of a significant moment, the summoning-up of time and experience. They make extravagant use of gardens, do artists, they individualize them—a Monet garden is a world away from a Van Gogh garden—the garden may shape their work, but their gardens also shape our perception of the garden, of plants and flowers, so that, once seen, a particular painting will forever influence our own vision: reality is affected by metaphor.

There does seem to be some kind of parallel between the ways in which writers and painters use gardens and garden imagery. The reality garden invites use as metaphor, for a novelist—to suggest mood, climate, personality—while for the painter intense study can influence and determine presentation, the discovery of a personal vision—the garden expressing the painter's own perception. A metamorphosis, perhaps, rather than a metaphor, but in each case the real garden has undergone a sea-change, either as language or as paint on a canvas. And I found it particularly interesting to discover how many painters were applied gardeners. Chocolate earth under the fingernails for Virginia Woolf, but also for Monet, Bonnard, Matisse, Klee.

The Written Garden

"Last night I dreamt I went to Manderley again." The open-ing line of Daphne du Maurier's *Rebecca*, and she goes on to evoke the dreamed garden: "The rhododendrons stood fifty feet high, twisted and entwined with bracken, and they had entered into alien marriage with a host of nameless shrubs . . . Ivy held prior place in this lost garden, the long strands crept across the lawns, and soon would encroach upon the house itself . . . Nettles were everywhere, the van-guard of the army. They choked the terrace, they sprawled about the paths, they leant, vulgar and lanky, against the very windows of the house." There are several pages of this, and you know where you are at once: the garden as image of decay and destruction, of time passing. And with sug-gested menace. We read with a shiver of anticipation, though the garden-minded reader will itch to get going with secateurs and strimmer.

This is a garden—albeit a dreamed garden—used with intent, conjured up with fictional purpose to serve as atmos-pheric ingredient in the story. Manderley and its surround-ings on the Cornish coast are almost an extra character in Du Maurier's powerful novel. The narrator (we never learn her name—an odd authorial gimmick) is the young bride of the glamorous Maxim de Winter, and arrives there to find a cli-mate of mystery and oppression—the sinister housekeeper, the pervading memory of the dead first wife, Rebecca, and the narrator's obsessive belief that Maxim is in permanent mourning for her and that she can never take Rebecca's place. When first she arrives at Manderley with Maxim, rhododendrons are brought into service: "We were amongst the rhododendrons. There was something bewildering, even shocking, about the suddenness of their discovery . . . They startled me with their crimson faces, massed one upon another in incredible profusion, showing no leaf, no twig, nothing but the slaughterous red, luscious and fantastic, unlike any rhododendron plant I had seen before." Rebecca had been a vibrant dark beauty, and when the narrator first uses the morning room, Rebecca's personal space, she finds it filled with rhododendrons, rich and glowing, used as cut flowers in this room and no other; they are uncomfortable, assertive, suggestive.

Manderley is a Jacobean mansion, modeled in part on Menabilly, the Cornish house in which Du Maurier lived for many years. Perhaps there were rhododendrons there, an inspirational prompt, and a correct one—they do well in the West Country climate and soil, and require the extensive grounds of some substantial mansion. Nothing hesitant or unassuming about the rhododendron, and they seem an appropriate image for the haunting presence of the dead Rebecca—flamboyant, luxuriant, confident.

The fictional garden of intent needs to be skillfully and knowledgeably planted. Daphne du Maurier knew what she was about with those rhododendrons, and the dreamed garden is entirely persuasive. Those nettles; the ivy. Ivy is definitely the novelist's plant of choice; as soon as ivy sneaks in you know it is there with possibly sinister intent. Elizabeth Bowen has a story called "Ivy Gripped the Steps," in which a middle-aged man returns to the south coast town in which, as a small boy, he frequently stayed with a friend of his mother, a widow who lived in the abandoned house at which he gazes as the story opens: "Ivy gripped and sucked at the flight of steps, down which with such a deceptive wildness it seemed to be flowing like a cascade. Ivy matted the door at the top and amassed in bushes above and below the porch. More, it had covered, one might feel consumed, one entire half of the high, double-fronted house . . . To crown all, the ivy was now in fruit, clustered over with fleshy pale green berries. There was something brutal about its fecundity."

The story is about the boy's experience in that house, back in the early years of the twentieth century, observing and not comprehending adult behavior, absorbing the culture of the genteel, leisured town, in which people are occupied with the expenditure of wealth, and in which, "Best of all, there were no poor to be seen." The subject matter is deception, the harm done to a child's emotional life, and the shadow of approaching war. In a subsequent war—the Second World War—the town had been on the front line, the house requisitioned, that way of life gone for ever. And the ivy nicely sums it all up, with an exaggerated use of words: "consumed," "brutal." Time, and events, have destroyed a society, a child's expectations and assumptions.

What kind of ivy, one wonders? Not elegant, well-behaved "Goldheart," I think. Definitely one of those large-leafed leathery thugs that should not be on offer in garden centers without a health-and-safety warning. I know all about those; I have one, planted in all innocence, and now it swarms an extra three or four feet up a wall each year, and requires attack by a hired garden firm. Though I allow it to stay because robins nest in it, and ivy is the food plant of the holly blue caterpillar, and I love to see those first sky-blue butterflies in early summer. And this is reality ivy, rather than fictional, so I do not have to consider its implications. Though the proliferation of urban ivy does make me think, looking around neighboring gardens, that if the human race vanished from London it is the ivy that would rapidly take over, swarming, consuming . . . And the foxes.

I suspect that Elizabeth Bowen was a gardener, though I can't find any biographical confirmation. But she frequently gives fictional space to gardens, or flowers, and with intent. In another story, it is the rose that sets the tone. "Each side of the path, hundreds of standard roses bloomed, over-charged with colour, as though this were their one hour. Crimson, coral, blue-pink, lemon and cold white, they disturbed with fragrance the dead air. In this spellbound afternoon, with no shadows, the roses glared at the strangers, frighteningly bright."

All is not well here, we at once suspect, and indeed it is not. "Look at All Those Roses" has a couple suffer a car breakdown; the wife is given tea at the house of the roses while her husband goes in search of help. Her hostess is an odd, bleak woman; there is a paraplegic child, a girl who makes precocious comments. Nothing is explained, there are just disturbing hints. And the glaring roses.

Standard roses, you note, placing them very much within

a context. The standard rose is pretty well a dead duck now-adays, though Elizabeth Bowen wasn't concerned with the rose as a style symbol (more on that in a later section). Her roses are scene-setters, pure and simple, and elsewhere she can flourish a garden to define the personality of its owner. In her novel *The Little Girls*, she plunges the reader into a garden with "steamy flower-smells . . . spongy serpentine grass path . . . Mauve, puce and cream-pink stocks . . . blue-bronze straggling profusion of catmint. Magnificent gladioli staggered this way and that . . . she was an exuberant, loving, confused and not tidy gardener . . . Roses were . . . squandering petals over cushions of pansies . . . dahlias grew: some dwarf, some giant, some corollas like blazons, some close-fluted, some velvet, some porcelain or satin." We get a clear picture of the person who would have such a garden, and there is a period touch here also (the book is set in the 1920s)—the staggering gladioli and the range of dahlias. The discriminating dahlia grower of today sticks to those small-headed free-flowering kinds, preferably that scarlet one called "Bishop of Llandaff." But the range quoted tells me also that Elizabeth Bowen knew a thing or two about dahlias.

It is nicely appropriate that two of our best-known children's books feature gardens—*The Secret Garden* and *Tom's Midnight Garden*, though to very different ends. Frances Hodgson Burnett's *The Secret Garden* was first published in book form in 1911 (as a serial in 1910). She was by then an established author, already a bestseller with her *Little Lord Fauntleroy*. The garden of *The Secret Garden* is an abandoned walled garden into which the child Mary, the story's protagonist, finds her way: "It was the sweetest, most mysterious-looking place any one could imagine. The high walls which shut it in were covered with the leafless stems of climbing roses which were so thick that they were matted together . . . All the ground was covered with grass of a wintry brown and out of it grew clumps of bushes which were surely rose-bushes if they were alive. There were numbers of standard roses which had so spread their branches that they were like little trees. There were other trees in the garden, and one of the things which made the place look strangest and loveliest was that climbing roses had run all over them and swung down long tendrils which made light swaying curtains, and here and there they had caught at each other or at a far-reaching branch and had crept from one tree to another and made lovely bridges of themselves."

Mary Lennox is a ten-year-old orphan who has been sent from India, where she was born, into the care of her guardian uncle at Misselthwaite Manor in Yorkshire. He is absent, and Mary finds herself alone there with the housekeeper and servants. She is a child who has been neglected by her parents but indulged by Indian servants, and is as a result spoiled and self-centered. The theme of the book is regeneration—the regeneration of Mary by those at the Manor and beyond who are constructively kind to her, the recovery of Colin, a hysterical invalid who, she discovers, is the other child resident at the Manor, the ten-year-old son of the absent Mr. Craven. And, symbolically, the recovery of the garden, which is the site of the death of Mr. Craven's wife, and the reason for its abandonment. He returns, and sees the restored garden: "The place was a wilderness of autumn gold and purple and violet blue and flaming scarlet and on every side were sheaves of late lilies standing together—lilies which were white or white and ruby. He remembered well when the first of them had been planted that just at this season of the year their late glories should reveal themselves. Late roses climbed and hung and clustered and the sunshine deepening the hue of the yellowing trees made one feel that one stood in an embowered temple of gold."

So this is a story heavy with significance—that children will behave according to the way in which they have been treated, that trauma can be overcome by the right kind of application, that fresh air and outdoor activity are good for you. Perhaps that is why I don't at all care for it; the book seems from the start too heavily and obviously loaded with meaning, and sentimental with patches of whimsy. But many will disagree; the book has been widely admired, and is seen as a seminal children's classic. It is very much of its time—the emphasis on healing through the power of positive thinking came from the Christian Science movement, in which Frances Hodgson Burnett was interested. And the crucial importance of fresh air was a central tenet of early-twentieth-century childcare. It hung on, indeed, until mid-century. I can remember parking the baby in her pram out in the garden in midwinter, because that was what the baby books said you should do. All that is fair enough; what puts me off is the way in which the beliefs are expressed, with the idea of a kind of "magic" for which the main vehicle is an extremely tiresome robin, who invites several pages of whimsical writing.

The concept of the garden, on the other hand, is fine, and

convincingly realized. Ann Thwaite, Frances Hodgson Burnett's biographer, has pointed out that she was an active and practical gardener, and she herself wrote: "I love to kneel down on the grass at the edge of a flower bed and pull out the weeds fiercely and throw them into a heap by my side. I love to fight with those who can spring up again almost in a night and taunt me. I tear them up by the roots again and again . . ." And the secret garden descriptions are nicely precise, as an account of what happens to an abandoned garden, and also of its rejuvenation: the pruning of the roses convincingly accurate.

The garden of *The Secret Garden* is a therapeutic garden. Half a century separates its publication from that of Philippa Pearce's *Tom's Midnight Garden*, which could not be more different, and the central distinction lies in the voice, the tone of the book. *The Secret Garden* has that characteristic Edwardian note of patronage, the arch tone of the period (escaped by some, notably Edith Nesbit), writing *down* to children. Philippa Pearce comes from another age of children's literature and the writing of *Tom's Midnight Garden* is unaffected, a pure and direct narrative voice. And the garden is a dreamed garden, a garden that no longer exists, in the time of the story, but is the wonderful catalyst for a fantasy about the nature of time. Tom Long has been sent to stay during the summer holidays with an uncle and aunt, because his brother has measles. The uncle and aunt live in an apartment which is part of the conversion of a large, old house, in the hall of which is a grandfather clock that Tom hears strike thirteen, as he lies awake at midnight. He steals downstairs to inspect it, and finds that a door opens into a garden, where by day there had been nothing but a yard with dustbins: "... a great lawn where flowerbeds bloomed; a towering fir-tree, and thick, beetle-browed yews that humped their shapes down two sides of the lawn; on the third side, to the right, a greenhouse almost the size of a real house; from each corner of the lawn, a path that twisted away to some other depths of garden, with other trees."

And so it all begins. A little girl appears in the garden—Hatty—and Tom is no longer alone but is joined every night by this pinafored playmate. Hatty is an orphan, treated coldly by the aunt with whom she lives in this house, and teased by her three older boy cousins (an orphan is the recurring figure in children's literature—every child's worst fear made manifest, but the status ameliorated by the story); she welcomes Tom (always in his pajamas) and shows him her secret hiding places: "a leafy crevice between a wall and a tree-trunk, where a small human body could just wedge itself; a hollowed-out centre to a box-bush, and a run leading to it—like the run made in the hedge by the meadow; a wig-wam shelter made by a rearrangement of the bean-sticks . . ." As the story continues, Tom and Hatty stray beyond the confines of the garden to the meadow and the river beyond, but always the garden is central, the place into which Tom escapes each night, the place where Hatty can join him: "He saw the garden at many times of its day, and at different seasons; its favourite was summer, with perfect weather. In earliest summer hyacinths were still out in the crescent beds on the lawn, and wallflowers in the round ones. Then the hyacinths bowed and died; and the wallflowers were uprooted, and stocks and asters bloomed in their stead.

There was a clipped box bush by the greenhouse, with a cavity like a great mouth cut into the side of it; this was stacked full of pots of geraniums in flower. Along the sundial path, heavy red poppies came out, and roses; and, in summer dusk, the evening primroses glimmered like little moons."

The apartment at the top of the house is occupied by its landlady, an old lady called Mrs. Bartholomew. And when, at the end of the story, Tom meets her, after his last excursion with Hatty, when she has become strangely older, a young woman, everything falls into place: "... nothing stands still, except in our memory," Mrs. Bartholomew tells Tom; the memory garden that has stayed always the same in her dreams, and in Tom's. Both concepts are beautiful—the dreamed garden, which cannot become a yard with dustbins so long as it lives on in her memory, and the little girl who also lives on because a person—an old woman—is not just now, but also then, all the incarnations of herself. For the boy Tom, this is a moment of maturity, a glimpse of continuity and of growing up, and a reason why *Tom's Midnight Garden* is one of the greatest children's books of all time. But, above all, it is a narrative of great elegance, simply told, and leaving you with insights into the nature of time, and memory. It nicely complements W. H. Auden's comment in an essay on *Alice in Wonderland*: "There are good books which are only for adults, because their comprehension presupposes adult experiences, but there are no good books which are only for children."

The garden as therapy—*The Secret Garden*. And gardening as an activity can be therapeutic also, or rather, gardening advice. This proposal is neatly wound into *The Stone Diaries*, Carol Shields's finest novel, both as a story element and an opportunity to display one of the novel's several narrative devices whereby the life of Daisy Goodwill, born in Manitoba in 1905, is told: "Dear Mrs. Green Thumb, Your piece on hollyhocks was terrif. I liked the part about 'their frilled dirndl skirts' and their 'shy fuzzy stems.'" After the death of her husband, Daisy has taken on his horticultural column in the *Ottawa Recorder* to startling effect. Housewife and mother, it is the first time that Daisy has either earned some money herself, or displayed talent and received praise; she finds some much-needed self-esteem. She is devastated when, in due course, she is ousted by a regular journalist on the paper, but before this happens her readers have been rewardingly appreciative:

"... I laughed till I cried about your struggle with your leggy poinsettia."

"... just wanted to let you know your column on Chicago gardens pushed my husband's magic button."

"At last, someone's solved my black leg problem. Any advice on thrips?"

"... Loved 'Getting tough with phlox' ... bought an extra copy for my sister-in-law in Calgary who'll get a real kick out of it."

"Wow, you really told it like it is in 'Plant Food—Yes or No.' My wife and I have been bickering over this particular issue for years."

The Stone Diaries is a kaleidoscopic novel, brilliantly and intricately told by way of straight narrative, alternating points of view, letters, newspaper reports. The account of

Daisy's rather bleak married life is obliquely told, but there is a sudden vivid rush of words when it comes to the description of her garden and the later significance for Daisy of becoming the respected "Mrs. Green Thumb" is the more apparent: "And her lilacs! Some people, you know, will go out and buy any old lilac and just poke it in the ground, but Mrs. Flett has given thought to overall plant size and blossom color, mixing the white 'Madame Lemoine' lilac with soft pink Persian lilac and slatey blue 'President Lincoln.' These different varieties are 'grouped,' not plopped. At the side of the house a border of blue Sweet William has been given a sprinkling of bright yellow coreopsis, and this combination, without exaggeration, is a true artist's touch. Clumps of bleeding heart are placed—placed, this has not just happened—near the pale blueness of campanula; perfection! The apple trees in the back yard are sprayed each season against railroad worm so that all summer long their leaves throw kaleidoscopic patterns on the fine pale lawn. Here the late sun fidgets among the poppies. And the dahlias!"

Reading that, let alone the readers' letters, I don't need to know if Carol Shields was a gardener—I know she was. Only an informed gardener could have written that. In fact, it is something I *should* know; Carol was a friend, but I don't remember that we ever had a gardening conversation on our too rare meetings—the Atlantic usually between us. And, reading that passage again, I find myself wondering if she is describing some garden of her own. The blue Sweet William puzzles me—here, it is usually pink, red, white. And what on earth is railroad worm? (Ah—I think what is meant is the blue phlox—wild Sweet William, *Phlox divari-cata*, native to North America, and the railroad worm is the larva of a beetle, called the apple maggot this side of the Atlantic.)

The fictional garden is one aspect of the written garden. There is also the garden writing that is free of fictional purpose, concerned only with discussion, advice, celebration—the writing of those who garden. And the range and variety is extraordinary, from the briskly informative to the florid and pretentious. If we take a look at a few of them, it might be significant to start by going back over a century to someone who was writing in fact at the same time as William Robinson and Gertrude Jekyll, but could not be more different.

Elizabeth von Arnim's *Elizabeth and Her German Garden* was published in 1898 and was a huge success at the time—twenty-one editions by 1899. It was her first book, and she went on to write many novels, and indeed *Elizabeth and Her German Garden* was termed a novel, though it is no such thing. It is an account of her life as the chatelaine of a Prussian estate at Nassenheide in Pomerania, and especially of her creation there of a garden. She had been born in Sydney, but brought up in England, and had met and married a Prussian count fifteen years older than herself when twenty-three. After a few years in Berlin, he took her to live at the family estate, from which he was frequently absent on business, leaving her with an entourage of servants and estate workers. She seems to have been quite comfortable with his absences, found her surroundings idyllic, and set about creating a garden out of a wilderness—the place had been neglected for years.

I find *Elizabeth and Her German Garden* a tricky read. It is soaked in whimsical humor, mostly written with that arch tone that was perhaps appealing in 1898 but not to the twenty-first-century ear. Her husband is archly called the Man of Wrath, and her three children the April baby, the May baby and the June baby. There are whimsical vignettes of visiting eccentrics. But when she writes about the garden, her plans, her successes and her failures, it is another matter—a whiff of affectation here and there, but mainly it is her enthusiasm and enjoyment that come across. On first arrival she was rapturous about what she found: "There are so many bird-cherries round me, great trees with branches sweeping the grass, and they are so wreathed just now with white blossoms and tenderest green that the garden looks like a wedding. I never saw such masses of them; they seem to fill the place. Even across a little stream that bounds the garden on the east, and right in the middle of the cornfield beyond, there is an immense one, a picture of grace and glory against the cold blue of the spring sky."

The bird cherry she refers to is *Prunus padus*, native to northern Europe and northern Asia, also called the hackberry, or Mayday tree. The flowers grow in racemes, and I have never seen one; I had thought at first she meant our own *Prunus avium*, the native cherry that got A. E. Housman going: "Loveliest of trees, the cherry now/Is hung with bloom along the bough." Hers sound lovely too.

Elizabeth revels also in the existing wild growths: "... under and among the groups of leafless oaks and beeches were blue hepaticas, white anemones, violets and celandines in sheets. The celandines in particular delighted me with their clean, happy brightness, so beautifully trim and newly varnished, as though they too had had the painters at work on them . . . And then . . . came the lilacs—masses and masses of them . . . one great continuous bank of them . . . away down as far as one could see, shining glorious against a background of firs."

But a garden is what she wants, and on a considerable scale, given the acreage at her disposal. She plants sweet peas, hollyhocks, Madonna lilies and, above all, she sets about ordering and planting roses. Roses are to be her specialty, and she names them all, meticulously: "Marie van Houtte," "Viscountess Folkestone," "Mme Laurette Messimy," "Souvenir de la Malmaison," "Devoniensis," "Persian Yellow," "Duke of Teck" . . . and so on until she has listed nineteen, a splendid litany of rose names. Remarkably, every single one is still available, I find; they have hung on, continuously cultivated for over a hundred years, demonstrating the tenacity of a good rose. Though some are clearly rarities now; you would have to pursue the right supplier. Back in Elizabeth's day, she would have been scouring the cursory printed nurserymen's catalogs that I remember my grandmother receiving, somber text listing plant name and price with never an image in sight, a world away from the lavish photography and extravagant descriptions that we are used to today. Plant catalogs now compete with the garden center in enticement technique. They reach for superlatives: fantastic, stunning, gorgeous, spectacular, fabulous, luscious, eye-catching. The images are always of plant perfection; eyeing them, you forget about the normal garden defects—the dead-heads, the mildew, the black spot, the greenfly.

Elizabeth was a complete novice when it came to gardening. She makes plenty of mistakes, struggles with dry, light soil that is particularly hostile to roses, has her failures: "The long border, where the rockets were, is looking dreadful. The rockets have done flowering, and, after the manner of rockets in other walks of life, have degenerated into sticks . . . the giant poppies I have planted out in them in April have either died off or remained quite small, and so have the columbines." But what is endearing, and impressive, about her, is that she had an eye, a vision, she knew what she wanted, and that was quite out of kilter with the gardening fashion of the day. She wanted irregularity, groupings, drifts of spring plantings, foxgloves and mulleins shining in her wild shrubbery walks. She is frustrated at every turn by her gardener, who wants everything in straight rows: ". . . he went about with a long piece of string making parallel lines down the borders of beautiful exactitude and arranging the poor plants like soldiers at a review." And it is at this point that one learns the main source of her frustration: "If I could only dig and plant myself!" It would have been quite out of the question, it seems, for a Prussian lady of the manor to set to with spade and fork herself. Once, she does slink off furtively with spade and rake to sow some morning glory, retreating in haste to her chair "to save my reputation . . . it is a blessed sort of work, and if Eve had had a spade in Paradise and known what to do with it, we should not have had all that bad business of the apple."

How odd. There was Gertrude Jekyll, at the same time, digging away happily in England without inviting social outrage, but apparently in Prussia they did things differently. Eventually, it all got too much for Elizabeth, and she moved to England, with the oppressive Prussian husband dying in 1910. She went on to become an established writer, have an affair with H. G. Wells, marry Earl Russell (brother of Bertrand) and entertain a host of friends at the home she set up in Switzerland. She mixed with the literati of the day—Katherine Mansfield was a cousin, and both E. M. Forster and Hugh Walpole served as tutors to her children at Nassenheide. Forster later claimed that he hadn't been able to find the garden, that it was more of a park, but one feels he can't have looked very hard. Those hundreds of roses? She sounds rather attractive—tiny, only five foot, vivacious and gregarious. She died in America in 1941 and apparently her gravestone bore the epitaph, chosen by herself: *parva sed apta*—small but to the point. One has to forgive the coy style of the non-gardening parts of *Elizabeth and Her German Garden* as the expected feminine note of the day, made up for by the genuine fervor of her gardening voice, and her avant-garde ideas. She wanted a white garden, anticipating Vita Sackville-West by fifty years, and planned a yellow border: "There are to be eschscholtzias, dahlias, sunflowers, zinnias, scabiosa, portulaca, yellow violas, yellow stocks, yellow sweet peas, yellow lupins . . . I want it to be blinding in its brightness after the dark cool path through the wood." It sounds mad, a wild hotchpotch planting, but I like the innovative enthusiasm.

I started my grown-up reading life in the age of the

Sitwells—Osbert, Edith and Sacheverell; the late 1940s and early 1950s. Their works were the required reading matter of the day; every intellectually aspiring household had Osbert's four-volume autobiography on the book table, a volume of Edith's poetry, something of Sacheverell's vast output (art, architecture, music). I dipped in, dutifully, and realized that you discover your reading taste from what you don't care for quite as much as from what you enjoy. I couldn't be doing with this sort of thing: grandiloquent overwriting for the most part, the use of ten words where one would do, a general miasma of pretension. I didn't know that in fact the Sitwells were often under merciless attack at the time, figures of fun in some quarters, and indeed by the 1960s they had certainly fallen from favor and have slipped further and further from view ever since.

Osbert, Edith and Sacheverell were the children of Sir George Sitwell, of Renishaw Hall, in Derbyshire. Earlier Sitwells had made a fortune from landowning and iron-making, achieved a baronetcy in 1908, and built themselves the gothic pile, Renishaw. And this is where the garden writing comes in. Sir George Sitwell wrote a short book called *On the Making of Gardens*, in 1909, which is mainly about the Italian Renaissance, with some reflections on theories of garden landscaping. Its interest, for me, is that it concludes with a fine example of what can only be called patrician garden writing—unique, perhaps.

"It is not given to every man, when his life's work is over, to grow old in a garden he has made, to lose in the ocean roll of the seasons little eddies of pain and sickness and weariness, to watch year after year green surging tides of spring and summer break at his feet in a foam of woodland flowers, and the garden like a faithful retainer growing grey in its master's service. But for him who may live to see it, there shall be a wilder beauty than any he has planned. Nature, like a shy wood-nymph, shall steal softly back on summer nights to the silent domain, shading with tenderest pencilings of brown and grey the ripened stone, scattering wood-violets in the grassy alleys, and wreathing in vine and ivy the trellised arbour, painting with cloudy crusts of crumbly gold the long balustrades, inlaying the cornices with lines of emerald moss, planting little ferns within the fountain basin and tiny patches of green velvet upon the Sea-God's shoulder."

Osbert Sitwell wrote an introduction to a later edition of *On the Making of Gardens* which is respectful, though with slight misgivings about his father's prose style: "... couched in phrases often of stilted beauty ... fountains throughout are inclined to 'plash' ... a genuine period-piece." Well, yes, indeed. But *Elizabeth and Her German Garden* can also be said to be a period piece, and her writing could hardly be more violently different; apart from that winsome tendency, she appears by comparison agreeably unassuming and straight-forward. Sir George Sitwell had also created a garden, the Italianate garden at Renishaw, but, judging from his writing, one suspects that he did no actual gardening. That was what the faithful retainers were for. Elizabeth longed to get her hands dirty; he was too patrician to do so. Which makes him, for me, not a real garden writer but a garden commentator. Though interesting, as such, because that style is an indication of what focusing on a garden can do to a person. Well, to a certain kind of person.

So Sitwell deserves a mention for extremity of style only, not as a gardener writer. And Elizabeth von Arnim sneaks in just as honorary gardener: she *wanted* to get down there and dig, but was excluded on account of social status. The writing of the real gardener is another matter—the voices of those who really know what they are doing, the gardening connoisseurs, the gardening gurus.

Anna Pavord was the gardening pundit to whom I paid most attention from the time when she was first contributing regular garden articles to the *Independent*. Their attraction was that they were succinctly knowledgeable but in no way patronizing or dictatorial; she simply helped you, with her expertise and her illuminating suggestions about how to set out a border, or tackle some recalcitrant piece of terrain. I have her to hand still, by way of her *The Curious Gardener*, a calendar of the year in the garden, again a nice combination of practicality and imaginative commentary. She wanders off into accounts of gardens she has admired, of her plant-hunting travels, a forensic inspection of pests and what to do about them, a swipe at aspects of the Chelsea Flower Show: "... the humourless pretension of the flower-arranging tent. Here, tortured creations draped in chiffon bear as much relation to the garden as a plastic ketchup bottle." She is essential reading on the clematis or the hydrangea: you see at once what you are doing wrong by way of planting or pruning. And then there are her two major scholarly works. I shall be referring to *The Tulip* in a later section; *The Naming of Names* is a companion volume in terms of its marriage of erudition with an eminently readable pursuit of botanical history. Anna Pavord is the perfect instance of a gardener writer, one for whom gardens and gardening have been the prompt for substantial and elegant writing.

Way back, I remember relishing James Fenton's newspaper gardening articles. Fenton is of course an eminent poet, and I doubt if there have been many, or any, other poets with such a depth of practical horticultural knowledge. The articles were engagingly witty, and nicely instructive. I wish I had cut them out and kept them, but I have a whiff of them in the form of his brief book *A Garden from a Hundred Packets of Seed*, a selection of articles for the *Guardian*. Opening it at random, the signature style jumps out at me: "*Viola tricolor* 'Bowles' Black is the unanswerable self-seeder. Irrefutably black when grown in isolation it enjoys fooling around with other violas. Keen on bloodlines, are we? Then we should 'rogue out' the less perfectly black seedlings." Fenton made a garden outside Oxford, and I remember visiting when he was in the process of designing and laying it out. "There," he said, gesturing toward a sweep of bare earth, "is the laburnum walk. And there"— an area of dock, nettle and bramble—"is the Margery Fish garden."

Ah, Margery Fish. From time to time Josephine and I visit East Lambrook Manor Gardens in Somerset. The gardens were created by Margery Fish and her husband, Walter, after they bought the Manor in 1938, and are today restored much as they were when Margery died in 1969, and hold, incidentally, the National Collection of geraniums (hardy geraniums, this means). I am clocking up National Collections that I have managed to visit. Her book *We Made a Garden* is an account of what sounds the Herculean task of turning two acres of former farmyard and rubbish deposit into an intricate area of winding paths, beds, walls, enclosed areas. And they did it themselves, she and her husband, hauling stone, clearing away "old beds, rusty oil stoves, ancient corsets, pots, pans, tins and china, bottles and glass jars . . ." Her account is practical and informative: if you want to know how to create a lawn where lawn there never was, go to Margery Fish. And also both inspirational and attractively candid. Inspirational in that it is full of plant references and descriptions of what they did; why on earth have I never had Dresden China daisies, I find myself thinking crossly, or a terrace garden (too late for that, but *Bellis perennis* "Dresden China"—might just be in time there), and candid in its references to a prime instance of marital gardening discord. Not all the time—Walter Fish was largely responsible for the hard landscaping, and she seems to have deferred to his skill and energy in that respect, but when it came to plant preferences and gardening practice she was in a state of constant negotiation. Indeed, there is a subtext of forbearance throughout the book; I find myself not much caring for Walter. His taste was for large, showy stuff, with a passion for dahlias, and no interest in the winter or spring garden, just the display of high summer. Margery favored the less flamboyant, the more subtle—the euphorbias, the hellebores, the hardy geraniums, the astrantias, vincas, snowdrops, aquilegias, pulmonarias. And I'm right behind her, remembering the garden as I have seen it in spring and early summer. Walter used to trample all over "her" plants when planting out his precious dahlias (the loudest and flashiest possible), and where his gardening manners were concerned he sounds exasperating—never picking up his prunings or dead-heads but leaving them for her to clear away. Like some men in the kitchen—cooking without doing their washing up. Still, it was a gardening partnership, if a sometimes edgy one, and Margery Fish is herself in the front ranks of gardening writers.

The attraction of writing like hers is its unpretentious simplicity. Remember Sir George Sitwell? She is not thinking of herself as writer, but as gardener. She writes out of passionate addiction, and expertise, but the writing is straightforward, unselfconscious. The same can be said of Beth Chatto, distinguished especially for her writing of difficult gardening circumstances—gardening where it is wet, gardening where it is dry. She has written mainly of her (and her husband's) creation of five acres of garden in Essex, comprising gravel garden, woodland garden, water garden, and so forth. Her matter-of-fact, precise style can have me as absorbed as I would be reading skillful fiction, entirely involved in her account of compost-making (an activity in any case quite out of the question in my small paved London garden). Beth Chatto's *The Dry Garden* has me wanting to move at once to East Anglia, shed forty years, and start a new, robust gardening life with a garden full of artemisias, santolinas, eryngiums, grasses, all the Mediterranean things. The book is spattered with plant names; you need to read it with the omniscient iPad at hand: I see, that's what *Epimedium* × *versicolor* "Sulphureum" looks like. I find myself conjuring up a virtual-reality garden as I read. Bird books are the same sort of reading material, for me: every now and then I settle down with my *Field Guide to the Birds of Australia*—I shall never see a Splendid Fairy-wren again (I did once—they are sapphire blue) but I want to imagine it.

Marital gardening in this instance seems to have been an altogether more harmonious affair. Beth Chatto thanks her husband warmly—"whose life-long hobby has been to study the natural homes of our garden plants"—saying that without him neither a garden nor a book would have been possible. That's better. Casting a beady eye over these various gardening partnerships I can see that they work best where roles are tacitly defined—Andrew Chatto providing the scholarly ballast for a garden, Leonard Woolf as the acknowledged driving force, Harold Nicolson taking over the initial layout.

Both Margery Fish and Beth Chatto are restrained, meticulous, orderly in style. Eleanor Perényi stands in nice contrast; she was American, and her book *Green Thoughts* (1981) is wonderfully different—rambling, discursive, opinionated. She was married before the war to a Hungarian baron, and lived in his castle, with a 750-acre farm, forest, vineyard and distillery where alcohol was made from potatoes. She tried to garden there, in conflict with an alien gardening tradition (and herself noting a similarity with Elizabeth von Arnim), but her real gardening life began after she returned to America in 1940 (divorcing her husband in 1945), and worked as an editor on magazines such as *Harper's Bazaar*. She was living on the Connecticut coast, and so was confronted with the conditions imposed by that ferocious East Coast climate—the hot humid summers, the frost and snow of winter, and a challengingly short growing season. Spending many summers in those parts in the 1980s, with American friends, I used to admire their determination and tenacity in getting any sort of a garden going for the summer—the planting-out of annuals, and then the desperate efforts to protect them against what seemed every kind of onslaught, from the woodchucks that would dig them up to a wealth of chomping insects.

Green Thoughts is constructed in the form of alphabetical essays from "Annuals" to "Woman's Place," by way of compost, dahlias, earthworms, frost, herbs, ivy, mulches, poppies, seeds, toads, weeds and much else—episodic, sometimes briskly dismissive, sometimes chatty, impressively well informed. Eleanor Perényi ropes in everyone from Petrarch, Virgil, Alexander Pope to Henry James. She flings out opinions right and left, sometimes condemnatory; petunias, for instance, are "pretty, very pretty—and as hopelessly impractical as a chiffon ball dress. Rain soils and bedraggles them; they are mostly too short and floppy to make a good cut flower and need constant shearing if they are to bloom throughout a summer." There, so much for the petunia. She can be lofty in her views, on color, for instance: "Nature's favorite color is a washed-out magenta, the original shade (and the one their hybrids will revert to if they go to seed) of petunias, garden phlox, sweet peas, nicotiana, foxgloves . . . The preferred color of the unsophisticated is firehouse red, the winner among tulips, zinnias, dahlias, salvias, impatiens, begonias etc. by a wide margin. Orange and yellow come next, then pink, with blue and white, both comparatively rare in nature, last on the list . . . It follows that blue and white are the choices of the discriminating, and your real garden snob will go so far as to cast whole gardens as one or the other."

At this point I cast a nervous eye over my own garden, today in mid-June, to see where I stand: three different kinds of white roses, so I am in the clear there, blue campanula sprawling all over the place (and a choice white one in a pot), a white parahebe just opening out, a bowl of white impatiens to light up the shady side, but—oh dear—a pink trailing begonia, pink roses and red, not to mention a whole large pot of pink geraniums (but there is another pot of white, to compensate). That said, internal evidence in the book suggests that Eleanor Perényi did not by any means stick to this stark pronouncement, and, rather surprisingly, she admits to a weakness for dahlias—"and not the discreet little singles either."

Hers are "as blowzy as half-dressed Renoir girls; others are like spiky sea creatures, water-lilies, or the spirals in a crystal paperweight." She does not, I feel, have the Margery Fish taste for the subtle and unshowy, but wants the big and bold, and is explicit in her preference for blue: anchusa, perennial cornflowers—*Centauria montana*, echinops, the blue veronicas, monkshoods, catananches and, indeed, blue delphiniums (nothing more fiendish to control than the delphinium, set on falling over as soon as you turn your back). All the same, I would like to have seen her garden (you don't actually get much idea of it from the book), and I enjoy the way she dives into a subject that interests her—roses, herbs—truffling away for arcane information. *Green Thoughts* is a conversation, in effect, and like all good conversation is alternately witty, arresting, and sometimes usefully enlightening. She is excellent on compost-making; what is it about compost that seems to generate a rush to the head in such diverse writers? She delves fascinatingly into the whole question of The Lawn, and one reads her lawn-making views with respect, knowing well that a New England lawn requires unparalleled dedication, whereas over here grass just . . . grows. The book skips from instruction to forays into the history of the tulip, or the hybridization of roses; its charm lies in its arbitrary nature, and you find yourself reading in the appropriate way—dipping in, leafing through, becoming absorbed where you had no idea you would be interested.

A splendidly different gardening voice is that of Karel Čapek, in his *The Gardener's Year* (1929). Čapek was a Czech writer—playwright, essayist, writer of science fiction before that genre really took off. It reminded me at once of *The Good Soldier Schweik*, so this must be idiosyncratically Czech humor. *The Gardener's Year* is Čapek's *jeu d'esprit* about the perversity of gardening, written with wry humor. The garden, for Čapek, is an adversary, a cherished adversary perhaps, but nevertheless the awkward place where the gardener is forever on the back foot. Literally, more or less: "Gardeners have certainly arisen by culture and not by natural selection. If they had developed naturally they would look differently; they would have legs like beetles, so that they need not sit on their heels, and they would have wings, in the first place for their beauty, and, secondly, so that they might float over the beds. Of course, at a passing glance from a distance you don't see anything of a gardener but his rump, everything else, like head, arms, and legs, is hidden underneath." Čapek's gardening year sets out with the assumption that the weather is always wrong, whatever it is doing, and is the second adversary, after the garden itself. He is not so much advising the reader, as warning; there is a tacit agreement that a garden is indeed a lovesome thing, but don't for one moment imagine that it is achieved other than by way of gargantuan struggle. Take the simple matter of watering: "... until it has been tamed a hose is an extraordinarily evasive and dangerous beast, for it contorts itself, it jumps, it wriggles, it makes puddles of water, and dives with delight into the mess it has made, then it goes for the man who is going to use it and coils itself round his legs." He discusses the question of soil improvement: "The garden . . . consists mainly of special ingredients such as earth . . . stones, pieces of glass, mugs, broken dishes, nails, wire, bones, Hussite arrows, silver paper from slabs of chocolate . . ." I know what he means, having tackled the unreconstructed soil of a London back garden. Never mind, he persists; unable in his town garden to acquire "guano, leaves, rotten cow-dung," he "hunts about at home for eggshells, burns bones after lunch, collects his nail-cuttings, sweeps soot from the chimney." In July, he accepts the "immutable law" that roses should be grafted. Not something I have ever felt impelled to do, but pre-war Czech gardening must have been different. "When all is ready the gardener tries the blade of the knife on the tip of his thumb; if the grafting-knife is sufficiently sharp it gashes his thumb and leaves an open and bleeding wound. This is wrapped in several yards of lint, from which a bud, rather full and big, develops on the finger. This is called grafting a rose."

At one point he gets interested in urban vegetation in

general, urban flora, noting that "one kind of vegetation flourishes in coffee-houses, and another, shall we say, at pork-butchers; that some kinds and genera grow best at railway stations . . . it could be demonstrated, perhaps . . . that another flora flourishes outside the windows of Catholics, different from that outside the windows of unbelievers and freethinkers." As for window boxes: "There are two kinds: the poor and the rich. That with poor people is usually better; besides, with the rich it dies annually, while they are away for holidays."

You don't go to Čapek for gardening advice but for an entertainingly central European take on the challenge of the garden. That's what I like him for, and for being just as far as is possible from Sir George Sitwell, though I suppose I must be charitable and see Sitwell as a cultural product also. Equally embedded.

This has been a discussion of the written garden—two kinds of written garden, the fictional garden and the entirely non-fictional writing of those who know about gardening, the garden writers. I could of course have cited many more instances of both, but enough is enough; what I wanted to do was to explore contrasts, in both kinds of writing. The novelists (all women, I realize, and that was not deliberate—men will get a look-in later on) demonstrate, I feel, something of the flexibility of the garden as fictional material, of different ways of using it, not just as background in a story, but as rather more than that—a story element, an essential feature. And my chosen gardener writers are various also, but each of them fired into print, as it were, by their gardening addiction. Essential reading matter for any gardener, indeed for anyone.

The Fashionable Garden

Like most people, I have gardened according to the fashion, or the taste, of the day. I have hunted down dwarf conifers and then ripped them out a few years later; I have junked gladioli and substituted crocosmia, preferably *Crocosmia* "Lucifer"; I can barely remember staking chrysanthemums and storing dahlia tubers. Restricted now to my few square yards of London garden, I can't go for broke with *Verbena bonariensis* all over the place, or alliums, or penstemons. I did have a bed of *Euphorbia amygdaloides*, but the local foxes lounged on it all the time, so it has been replaced with ground-cover roses, which have nicely dispersed the foxes.

These days, garden fashion is dictated by television gardening programs, by garden journalism, by what is available and conspicuous in garden centers. Both television and garden centers are relatively recent dictators—neither was around when I first took an interest in gardening in the 1960s. But we have always gardened according to the written word, and some very persuasively written words at that. In the early part of the twentieth century, and back in the nineteenth, writers were the garden gurus of the day. Not usually fiction writers, but devoted gardeners—maniacal gardeners, indeed—who turned themselves into writers in order to spread the message. Back in the 1970s, I planted a clematis up an old apple tree, as did many other readers of the *Observer*. We had been taking note of Vita Sackville-West's gardening articles. At the time, I knew little about Vita Sackville-West; her long poem *The Land* was on my shelves—a bestseller in its day but now entirely unregarded. Its companion volume, *The Garden*, I had somehow missed out on. I did not know that she had been the lover of Virginia Woolf and many others, that she had been a figure of scandal and interest in her time. Her novels were no longer around. I had heard of Sissinghurst, her famous garden, and read the gardening pieces with attention; I just thought she was an upper-class lady with some interesting gardening ideas. As indeed she was, and her style probably did more to affect a certain kind of gardening—middle-class gardening, I suppose—than anything for fifty years or more. Her readers rushed to get into trough-gardening, old roses, hellebores, blue flowers and white ones, climbers swarming up trees, and all small, subtle and quiet-colored flowers. We rooted up our hybrid teas and floribundas, we threw out the chrysanthemums and the cactus dahlias, we spurned anything with showy or outsize blooms. We aspired to a white garden. The circulation of the *Observer* soared, and the volume of letters to Vita from her readers required a special mail-van delivery to Sissinghurst.

She was indeed a talented gardener, though actually the design of the Sissinghurst garden apparently owed more to her husband, Harold Nicolson, who complained about her refusal to plan, to think ahead: "The tragedy of the romantic temperament is that it dislikes form so much that it ignores the effect of masses . . . She wishes just to jab in the things which she has left over." Ah, matrimonial gardening dissent, familiar to many of us. In fact, he was in charge of the hard landscaping, and she was the plantswoman. She was entirely self-taught, like many of the great gardening figures, and simply evolved her gardening style out of likes and dislikes, though she respected the professionals: "If you want real highbrow talk," she wrote, "commend me to three experts talking about auriculas. Bloomsbury is nothing to it. I couldn't understand half they said."

Vita's channel of influence was a newspaper. But the two greatest gardening influences of the early twentieth century came in book form. I have them both: Gertrude Jekyll's *Home and Garden* (1900) and William Robinson's *The English Flower Garden* (1883). They are my grandmother's copies, and I know that she gardened out of them; they lifted her, and countless others, out of the Victorian concept of gardening and into a new perception of how gardening could be—actually, one that we still favor.

William Robinson, an Irishman, came to England as a young man and found work at the Regent's Park Botanical Gardens in London, and within a few years was active as a garden writer, starting up his own journal, *The Garden*, in 1871, which, along with his two main publications, *The Wild Garden* (1870) and *The English Flower Garden*, served as the vehicle for his trenchant opinions and ground-breaking ideas: the new face of gardening. *The English Flower Garden* is a hefty polemic, full of swingeing pronouncements and persuasive advocacy of the Robinsonian theory of gardening, along with a great deal of robust practical advice and encyclopedic information. Robinson in hand, you need look no further. First and foremost, he was out to defy the Victorian craze for carpet bedding and seasonal planting. "Pastry-work gardening," he called it, and jeered at the typical garden of the day in which "only scarlet Geraniums, yellow Calceolarias, blue Lobelias or purple Verbenas were used ... the constant repetition of this scarlet, yellow and blue nauseating even those with little taste in gardening matters, while those with fine perceptions began to enquire for the Parsley bed by way of relief." Pungent stuff, and note the lofty reference to those with little taste in gardening matters. His sensitive readers will by now be in a panic, fearing to be among the damned, and will rush out to root up the bedding plants, and embark on the wild garden that Robinson is advocating—or rather, to instruct the gardeners to get going, because it is quite clear that Robinson is aiming at the more prosperous gardener, and supposes not only a substantial acreage but also an infrastructure of support. This is a far cry from the more egalitarian tone of today's garden writer, or television presenter.

The wild garden is, of course, no such thing. Robinson's grassy walks with swathes of spring bulbs, his stretches of grassland with specimen trees and naturalized plantings, his great borders of herbaceous plants and shrubs, were high maintenance. But they didn't *look* like it; they were the antithesis of the finicky particularity of Victorian gardening, in which everything was contrived and formalized. Robinson was after the natural look: "the best garden should arise out of its site and its conditions as happily as a primrose out of a cool bank." His illustrations extol the charms of informal cottage gardens (the well-heeled garden reader was to take a tip from those less well equipped, but with natural style), and he describes in minute detail how the Robinson effect is to be achieved. He effectively introduced the mixed or herbaceous border which has been a staple of gardens large and small ever since, that mixture of shrubs and hardy or half-hardy herbaceous flowers, densely planted, a long ripple of color and texture without the straight lines and patterning that he abhorred.

He was keen on the rock garden, a less happy feature as anyone who has tried to manage one finds out. The rock garden has rather disappeared today, except in botanical gardens where they have the skills and the labor to deal with these things, but they were still in favor in the 1970s, when I tried to make one. What happens, in practice, is that, having created your small hill of large rocks and earth, you plant up with alpine treasures and then find that every possible weed has snuck in and triumphantly shot its roots under the rocks, from where it is impossible to get them out. The alpines languish; the rock garden becomes a weed garden.

Robinson wanted diversity, an end to Victorian seasonal planting, but appreciation of the seasons by way of spring bulbs, woodland plants, winter-flowering shrubs. His wild garden supposed a merger of the garden with a wider land-scape of meadow and woodland. My grandmother had a shot at this, with a lawn that rolled down to a ha-ha above a pasture that was rimmed with copses, and grassy walks with naturalized narcissi, Robinsonian on a small scale only, but he would have approved. A ha-ha is the device favored in the eighteenth century whereby a lawn appears to merge with the landscape beyond by way of a sunken ditch below a retaining wall (the infinity swimming pool of today uses the same idea), the peculiar terminology said to suggest a person's surprise on discovering the deception—Ha! Ha!

With his distaste for "builders" and anything contrived, Robinson would be aghast at those television programs that turn a suburban garden into a building site and spend more time on pavilions, pavings and grottoes than on plants, or those Chelsea show gardens that are more about building materials than anything that grows. Though, that said, the Robinsonian wild garden influence hangs in with the popularity of the wild meadow, fiendishly difficult to establish and maintain—and the attempt by garden designers to cram the dying gasp of a wild garden into the toe of a narrow suburban plot.

Gertrude Jekyll wrote for Robinson's journal *The Garden*. She collaborated with him, indeed, and was sympathetic to his ideas, but she struck out on her own, was the esteemed garden designer of her day (a term she would have rejected—she called herself simply a gardener). She was the subject of that wonderful William Nicholson portrait, in which she is seen in profile, resembling Queen Victoria, and looking extremely cross—presumably wondering when this artist fellow will be done and she can get back to the garden. And there's the splendid companion study of her gardening boots: robust, black and purposeful. Her *Home and Garden* not only told its readers how to garden, but also how to arrange flowers, make potpourri and generally improve the home. Along with her many other books, *Home and Garden* is the ancestor of the glossy gardening books on sale today, most of them coffee-table fodder, and in many cases the size of coffee

tables, simply vehicles for lavish photography. But Jekyll—
and Robinson too—is literature by comparison. These are
books dense with text—confident, knowledgeable text.
Jekyll's black-and-white photos were her own work, while
Robinson's illustrations to *The English Flower Garden* are
engravings, if you please, done from original photographs of
the various seminal gardens he wished to cite.

We still garden according to Gertrude Jekyll, we still
favor her emphasis on gradations of color, her attention
to structural plants, her palette of blues and silvers and
whites. Her partnership with the much younger Edwin
Lutyens, the architect, married her plantings with his landscaping, and an emphasis on vernacular materials, very
much Arts & Crafts style. My grandmother raided their
schemes for her sunken rose garden, and the canal garden
where yew hedges enclosed a space around a long rill, with
ponds at each end. So did many others, in the early part of
the twentieth century; you still see the Jekyll/Lutyens look
up and down the land. She was formidably influential,
largely, I suppose, because like Robinson she was breaking
new ground—bringing to the garden ideas about color
massing and color combination which themselves owed
something to Impressionism. But this widespread influence
must have owed much also to her prolific output: the list of
her publications is startling—many books, and hundreds of
articles in *The Garden* and *Country Life* and elsewhere. All
this, and a life in the garden also—there is no question but
that she was out there and digging herself, those battered
portrait boots the perfect testimony. How did she do it? No
family, no children—though she pays nice attention to

children in *Home and Garden*, and has a book called *Children and Gardens*—and, of course, the early-twentieth-century middle-class domestic support system. She wouldn't have done the housework. And there would have been gardening staff as well. All the same, it is an amazing achievement for one woman—so much writing, so much garden designing (she designed around 400 gardens), all made possible by a lifetime spent out there in the garden experimenting with her own ideas.

There are those who decide gardening fashion, like Jekyll and Robinson, but there is also the matter of what plants are available. The nineteenth century was the great period of plant introduction, with intrepid plant hunters like David Douglas, Robert Fortune, Ernest Wilson and George Forrest bringing introductions from North America, the Himalayas, China, Japan. These effectively changed the face of gardening in this country, and the more arresting plants brought back at once became ferociously sought after, a garden must-have, like the handkerchief tree, *Davidia involucrata*, or the regal lily, *Lilium regale*—both from China. The Victorians may have been obsessed with carpet bedding, but they were also avid for the striking new acquisition, and by the beginning of the twentieth century the more affluent English garden must have looked very different from a hundred years before.

There had always been plant introductions, from Roman times onward, and conspicuously in the seventeenth century when the Tradescants, father and son, brought back from Russia, Virginia, and elsewhere, the plants that are garden staples today. In fact, if you make a forensic inspection of any garden now, there is little there that is native: our gardens are cosmopolitan, they speak in tongues. Introductions that may initially have been fashionable acquisitions for the few have become, over time, ubiquitous, and the norm.

If I consider especially cherished items in my own several gardens, they finger much of the rest of the world. In our first Oxfordshire garden, there was a fine *Robinia pseudoacacia*, called the black locust in North America from whence it comes, brought here by John Tradescant. Elegantly shaped, lightest of green leaves, racemes of white flowers—I loved it. Nearby, and nicely contrasting with its dark foliage, was a holm oak, *Quercus ilex*, which comes from the Mediterranean, so an interesting conjunction of two species which, in nature, would never have met. My beloved signature plant, *Erigeron karvinskianus*, comes from Mexico and is sometimes called Mexican fleabane, though I wouldn't dream of doing so. I don't know which plant hunter brought it here, but we are indebted—and indeed it has apparently spread pretty well all around the world, wherever conditions are appropriate, an opportunist migrant. I respect its independence; it doesn't care to be deliberately planted, it likes sites of its own choice, the cracks in a wall into which it slips.

Mexico has also supplied choisya, another favorite. I have recently had to take out a vastly overgrown *Choisya ternata* "Sundance," replacing it with *Hydrangea paniculata* "Limelight." So Mexico is elbowed aside by Asia. But I am not without a choisya. *Choisya* "Aztec Pearl" is flourishing, in a large pot. Elegant choice of name; I wonder if the Aztecs really did have it.

The longest-lived plant in my London garden is a corokia. It has been in the same large pot for over twenty years, terminally pot-bound, presumably, but apparently quite happy, lighting up the garden on sunny days with its little silvery leaves, studded with tiny yellow flowers in spring—tall, but see-through, so that it gives height without bulk. The corokias come from New Zealand, and mine (*Corokia cotoneaster*) is not seen around all that much, so that only a visiting New Zealand friend has been able at once to recognize and name it. Surprising that it can adapt so happily to life in a northern city.

I am addicted to fuchsias. Pot after pot of them; I have to avert my eyes from temptation, in the garden center—no, *not* another. So I am indebted to South America here, and that most evocative one of all, *Fuchsia magellanica*, apparently occurs right down to the tip of the continent, as the name suggests—evocative for me because there were great banks of it in my grandmother's garden, the red one and the pale pink. And Josephine has it, of course, in her Somerset garden. A family specialty, along with aquilegias, for which thanks to North America this time—allowed in all our gardens to self-seed and establish.

But my London garden is indebted to Japan, twice over. The *Hydrangea petiolaris*, the climbing hydrangea, is now swarming nicely over the back wall, though it took many years to get going. That comes from Japan and the Korean peninsula. And the *Fatsia japonica* that occupies the difficult bed on the shady side of the garden—established when I came here, so well over thirty years old now—is native to Japan and Taiwan. And to north London also, nowadays, you feel—you see it all over the place: robust, tolerant of city pollution.

Plant introductions influenced garden fashion, and new specimens would initially have been highly priced. But the most expensive plant ever was not so much a fashionable acquisition as an item of commerce. The Dutch tulip mania of the early seventeenth century is more an economic than a horticultural phenomenon. Tulipomania ran for just a few years, 1634–37, and at its height one of the most prized bulbs changed hands for a price equivalent to one of the then-finest houses on an Amsterdam canal. This was a specimen of the rare "Semper Augustus," which no longer exists but looks from contemporary paintings to have been an elegant white flower patterned with red striations. This patterning was the whole point: what was so sought-after was the "broken" tulip, where the normal plain coloring had become feathered with another color, as though delicately painted. It was unknown at the time why this mutation came about, and apparently it could not be induced, so that these unique "sports," when they occurred, caused great excitement among tulip growers which spread, at the time of the mania, to financial speculators. Each "broken" specimen was completely original, and remained that way, as did its offsets, though it did not produce offsets as freely as an ordinary bulb, so that they were slow to increase, enhancing their value even more.

Anna Pavord's definitive book *The Tulip* gives a fine account of this extraordinary incidence of economic madness, when sums far beyond the annual wage of the day were paid for a single dry brown "root," as the bulbs were called. They were sold when dormant, and since the cause and progress of this "breaking" was not understood, and it could not be induced, there was an element of chance which fueled the frenzied competition to acquire one of the treasured few. The right tulip was not just a status symbol—the ultimate fashion item—but had become, more importantly, a potential investment. If the "root" flowered as anticipated, it was even more valuable. All this seems quite extraordinary, viewed dispassionately today. A tulip stays in flower for just a couple of weeks or so, as would these have done, a brief and extravagantly expensive flourish.

The reason for the "breaking" was not in fact discovered until the 1920s. It is the result of a virus, caused by an aphid—the peach potato aphid—and today, when tulips are mass-marketed more as single-colored flowers, unwanted breaking can be prevented, though there are plenty of desirable bi-colored kinds around—parrot and viridiflora tulips. But in early-seventeenth-century Holland, when the phenomenon was mysterious, there were all kinds of desperate experiments to induce breaking; pigeon dung was thought to help, or plaster from old walls, chopping a red-flowered and a white-flowered bulb in half and binding them together, painting the tulip beds with the required color in powder paint. And of course sometimes these efforts would appear to have been successful, but no one knew the real reason.

We know what these horticultural aristocrats looked like from contemporary paintings. There were tulip books that were records of the collections held by tulip lovers, but there were also others that were effectively a magnificent sales catalog, the equivalent of the glossy brochure from today's nurserymen. These showed the expensive new "breaks," with their prices; the speculator had an image of what he could expect from his dry brown "root." But by 1637 the bubble had burst, prices plummeted, and the tulip reverted to being a much-cherished, much-valued garden asset, but no longer an object of commerce.

The tulip is native to Central Asia and Turkey, and it would seem that the basic reason for tulipomania occurring in Holland rather than anywhere else is that by the early seventeenth century there were tulips available in the Netherlands. The botanist Carolus Clusius had created a botanical garden at Leiden, importing a large stock of tulip bulbs, among the first to be known in western Europe, and observed the phenomenon of "breaking." So there were tulip bulbs to be bought—though at a price—making the tulip at once a status flower, an indicator of your wealth and taste, and then when it was realized that "breaks" were even more elegant and remarkable than the standard tulip, and something of a mystery, demand exceeded supply, and a flurry of economic madness ensued. The only time, I suppose, that an aphid has driven the stock market.

Tulips are indeed delectable. I prefer the smaller, more elegant species tulips to those armies of tall showy Darwin tulips—"Little Princess" is just going over as I write, underplanting an Acer in a big tub. And while not exactly two a penny today, they are not going to break the bank. Indeed the most expensive tulip I can find on the Internet is "Absalon" (dating from 1780, apparently), at £15.50 for three bulbs, which is indeed a "break"—brownish-purple feathered with yellow, and very handsome it looks.

Today, it would seem that the tulip has been ousted as the collectors' choice by the snowdrop. My favorite bulb supplier's snowdrop list includes plenty of single bulbs at £20, with "Tryzm" or "Phantom" going for £80. To the untutored eye they all look delightful—that exquisite graceful snowdrop combination of pure white and apple green—but very similar, though I can see that the subtle differences must be what entices the connoisseur. But these are cheap compared with the £725 paid elsewhere for *Galanthus woronowii* "Elizabeth Harrison," in 2012, which was in turn topped by the £1,390 raised for *Galanthus plicatus* "Golden Fleece" in 2015. That's more like it—still nowhere near tulip mania territory, but impressive cash for one small flower. And an instance presumably of botanical fervor rather than narrow-eyed financial speculation.

It is garden fashion that is under discussion here, and collecting is something of a side issue. That said, it is an intriguing pursuit, and there is something admirable about those people whose devotion to a single plant has had them end up with the National Collection of something—a garden with every conceivable kind of clematis, a garden that is bamboo from end to end. I can empathize, I can imagine doing it. I have never collected anything, except for a brief foray into samplers until antique shop samplers became too expensive, and anyway I was getting a bit bored with them, but I can absolutely see that you would never get bored with clematis, and that if there was one you hadn't tried, you would have to have it.

As we have seen, garden fashion depends on what there is available to become fashionable, and who is dictating garden style. It is also, of course, a matter of garden size, of grand gardening and substantial country-garden gardening and the skimpy urban or suburban plot. Grand gardening has been forever in a category of its own, from the Roman villa to the Victorian mansion complete with fern house, walled kitchen garden, orangery, hothouse with vines. And the stately home with serious acreage has been made over more comprehensively than any—more on that shortly. But the immemorial gardener with just a patch at the front and a bit more at the back has gardened without benefit of style advice or access to new introductions, and has gardened with what was to hand. Remember Gertrude Jekyll's fervent approval of the cottage garden. And what was to hand would have been, way back, the primroses (and snowdrops) you could take from the wild, and then all the ubiquitous, easily available marigolds and asters and nasturtiums and hollyhocks and pinks. And that lupin my neighbor down the road gave me a clump of, and the blue sweet pea from the seeds my mother sent, and my aunt's Michaelmas daisy, and Mrs. Smith's iris . . . Random, opportunistic, comfortingly referential—the personal element that a garden had before we acquired everything from the garden center and the catalog. And with fashion not an issue, except where a plant became more widely grown and available and so gradually seeped from the grander garden to any garden.

At no time was the garden owner more challenged by the requirements of contemporary fashion than in the late eighteenth century. The grand garden owner, that is, the landowner, the possessor of serious acreage. This was the age of "improvement," the age of Capability Brown and Humphry Repton. Jane Austen was poking fun at this obsession in *Mansfield Park*, when Mr. Rushworth declares his discontent with his unimproved seat:

"I wish you could see Compton," said he; "it is the most complete thing! I never saw a place so altered in my life . . . The approach *now*, is one of the finest things in the country: you see the house in the most surprising manner. I declare, when I got back to Sotherton yesterday, it looked like a prison—quite a dismal old prison."

"Oh, for shame!" cried Mrs Norris. "A prison indeed? Sotherton Court is the noblest old place in the world."

"It wants improvement, ma'am, beyond anything. I never saw a place that wanted so much improvement in my life; and it is so forlorn that I do not know what can be done . . . I must try to do something with it . . . but I do not know what. I hope I shall have some good friend to help me."

"Your best friend upon such an occasion," said Miss Bertram calmly, "would be Mr Repton, I imagine."

"That is what I was thinking of. As he has done so well by Smith, I think I had better have him at once. His terms are five guineas a day."

"Well, and if they were *ten*," cried Mrs Norris, "I am sure *you* need not regard it. The expense need not be any impediment. If I were you, I should not think of the expense. I would have everything done in the best style, and made as nice as possible."

Lancelot Brown—"Capability," from his practice of announcing the "capability," the potential, of a landscape—had got going by the middle of the eighteenth century, and by the time of his death in 1783 had had his way with estates including Chatsworth, Blenheim, Petworth and many others. He was a gardener by training, and honed his landscaping skills at Stowe, setting up his own business in due course, as both consultant and contractor. The general principle of his designs was simplicity, undulating ground with an expanse of grass reaching away to a lake or stream, clumps or belts of trees softening the contours of the land, all this sweeping away the clutter of formal gardens. If the contours were insufficiently pleasing, adjustments would be made—hills scooped aside, rivers dammed to create a lake—while grazing cattle would be kept away from the precincts of the mansion with a ha-ha. If there happened to be obtrusive buildings, a cottage or two, a whole village, then away with them also. A makeover by Brown was extensive, expensive, and essential if you were to make the grade as the modern landowner of an impressive estate.

In *Headlong Hall*, Thomas Love Peacock rolled Brown and Repton into one with his creation of Marmaduke Milestone, "a picturesque landscape gardener of the first celebrity":

"My dear sir," said Mr Milestone, "accord me your permission to wave the wand of enchantment over your grounds. The rocks shall be blown up, the trees shall be cut down, the wilderness and all its goats shall vanish like mist. Pagodas and Chinese bridges, gravel walks and shrubberies, bowling-greens, canals, and clumps of larch, shall rise upon its ruins. One age, sir, has brought to light the treasures of ancient learning; a second has penetrated into the depths of metaphysics; a third has brought to perfection the science of astronomy; but it was reserved for the exclusive genius of the present times, to invent the noble art of picturesque gardening, which has given, as it were, a new tint to the complexion of nature, and a new outline to the physiognomy of the universe!"

However, he is not without a critic. Sir Patrick O'Prism, another member of the house party of garrulous gentlemen whose opinions and exchanges are the substance of this plotless but engaging novel, takes issue: "I never saw one of your improved places, as you call them, and which are nothing but big bowling-greens, like sheets of green paper, with a parcel of round clumps scattered over them, like so many spots of ink, flicked at random out of a pen."

Peacock was writing in 1816, a couple of years after the publication of *Mansfield Park*, with both Brown and Repton safely out of the way, and the vogue for "improvement" itself perhaps ripe for some amiable derision. But Brown and Repton between them had worked on over 1,000 country estates, not all of them as majestic as Chatsworth or Blenheim, but ranging down to the homes of gentlemen of more modest situation anxious to make their acreage as up to date and impressive as possible.

Brown seems to have been a formidable personality, opinionated, a prolific writer, and an adept self-publicist. He died rich in 1783, having manipulated a great deal of English landscape, shifting inconvenient earth, and rearranging inappropriate water, and stamping his unforgettable name on some of the country's stateliest homes. Humphry Repton was his successor, broadly in sympathy with Brown's approach but keen to emphasize that landscape gardening should aim to display the natural beauty of the scene, and take pains to conceal any interference made to improve the natural state of the landscape: remove a hill, divert a stream, but this must not be apparent. He was concerned with architecture and a house to be displayed to best advantage by its setting. He reintroduced the terrace in front of a mansion, allowed an avenue approach, and permitted flower beds in the immediate vicinity of a house. He was not primarily a contractor, like Brown, though he would oversee a project if required, and was famed for his Red Books, customized for each client, in which a descriptive text was accompanied by paintings with flaps or overlays which showed the landscape around the property before his attentions and in the state they would be if the client followed his recommendations. The Red Book was, effectively, what he was selling, and he appears to have rivaled Brown in loquacity and a gift for self-presentation. His creation was the landscaped park as setting for a stylish mansion, as can be seen by his work at Uppark, Sheringham, Sezincote and other estates. Like Brown, he became the go-to operator for the aspirant home owner of means.

Tom Stoppard's glorious play *Arcadia*, a dance between past and present, is about truth and time, about Romantic and Classical, about Fermat's Last Theorem, about Byron, about love and sex, and it makes exquisite use of the eighteenth century's radical vision of landscape. The setting for the play is Sidley Park, in Derbyshire, and the action moves from the early nineteenth century to the present day, always in the same room, in which appear now the family in the past, now the family today, along with further essential characters including, in 1809, Mr. Noakes, described as "a landskip architect." Noakes lacks the Repton/Brown personality; he is a bumbling and sycophantic fellow, though equipped with a Repton-style Red Book, which gives Lady Croom pause for thought:

> LADY CROOM: . . . I would not have recognized my own garden but for your ingenious book—is it not?—look! Here is the Park as it appears to us now, and here as it might be when Mr Noakes has done with it. Where there is the familiar pastoral refinement of an Englishman's garden, here is an eruption of gloomy forest and towering crag, of ruins where there was never a house, of water dashing against rocks where there was neither spring nor a stone I could not throw the length of a cricket pitch. My hyacinth dell is become a haunt for hobgoblins, my Chinese bridge, which I am assured is superior to the one at Kew, and for all I know at Peking, is usurped by a fallen obelisk overgrown with briars—

In fact, it appears that what is to be made over, if Noakes secures his commission, is a Capability Brown "improvement." Hannah, a visiting academic in the present day, defines the ravaging of Sidley Park in terms of the shift from Enlightenment thought to the sensibilities of Romanticism.

HANNAH: . . . It's what happened to the Enlightenment, isn't it? A century of intellectual rigour turned in on itself. A mind in chaos suspected of genius. In a setting of cheap thrills and false emotion. The history of the garden says it all, beautifully. There's an engraving of Sidley Park in 1730 that makes you want to weep. Paradise in the age of reason. By 1760 everything had gone—the topiary, pools and terraces, fountains, an avenue of limes—the whole sublime geometry was ploughed under by Capability Brown. The grass went from the doorstep to the horizon and the best box hedge in Derbyshire was dug up for the ha-ha so that the fools could pretend they were living in God's countryside. And then Richard Noakes came in to bring God up to date. By the time he'd finished it looked like this . . . The decline from thinking to feeling, you see.

This is a most thought-provoking alignment of garden fashion with intellectual history, and earlier Hannah had had a go at perceived eighteenth-century derivative pretentiousness:

HANNAH: . . . English landscape was invented by gardeners imitating foreign painters who were evoking classical authors. The whole thing was brought home in the luggage from the grand tour. Here, look—Capability Brown doing Claude, who was doing Virgil. Arcadia! And here, superimposed by Richard Noakes, untamed nature in the style of Salvator Rosa. It's the Gothic novel expressed in landscape. Everything but vampires . . .

Repton was correcting Brown's undulations, clumps and belts of trees with the introduction of features that complied more with the current notion of the picturesque, and here the question of garden fashion merged with the wider problem of landscape appreciation—how the eighteenth-century person of taste was to view the world. Because it was not enough to view: the discriminating traveler must be able to discriminate between the picturesque, the beautiful and the sublime. And the picturesque was at the heart of the matter; ideally, a landscape should compose itself to the eye as does a painting by a master—Claude Lorrain and Salvator Rosa being particular favorites. To this end, fashionable travelers equipped themselves with a Claude glass, a small, slightly convex, tinted mirror. You turned your back on the scene to be assessed, in order to observe it reflected in the mirror, which would effectively abstract it from its surroundings, giving it a painterly, or picturesque, effect. Or not, as the case may be; if that particular section of the Lake District or wherever did not meet requirements, you moved on to find somewhere more satisfactorily picturesque. It seems to me very like today's tourist practice of taking a photograph before, or even without, looking at the object of interest.

These distinctions must have made travel even more taxing than it already was in the age of coach or horseback. You were in search of remarkable scenery, but must also be able to make an informed and intelligent pronouncement on the nature of the scenery in question. The discerning traveler would be able to summon up the appropriate response to the sublime. It had been defined, and distinguished from the beautiful, by Edmund Burke in 1757, in his *Philosophical*

Inquiry into the Origin of Our Ideas of the Sublime and the Beautiful, and was understood to imply an element of fear, and to involve majesty, vastness, the sense of awe and terror. The ocean was sublime, because of its implication of infinity. Equally, you could be comfortably (or uncomfortably) certain that you were in the presence of the sublime if viewing some great torrent of water, or intense and craggy cliffs.

The sublime was relatively straightforward, and the discerning traveler would be able to summon up the appropriate response. The trouble came with distinguishing the beautiful from the picturesque, the concept that had been established by William Gilpin with his publications on the nature of the picturesque in the later part of the century. It had become clear that scenic beauty alone was not enough, it must be possible also to find in the scene before you that painterly, picturesque quality, helped out, if necessary, by a Claude glass. And now, to complicate matters, the distinction was applied to more immediate scenery, to the landscape of a park or estate, whether improved or unimproved. The distinction had become a gardening matter.

That satirical fun could be had on this theme by Jane Austen, and Thomas Love Peacock indicates that the matter of the picturesque would have been familiar to most if not all their readers. Readers would have views themselves, in all probability, which might well have stemmed from familiarity with the work of Uvedale Price, a country landowner who made himself the principal spokesman on the subject in 1796, with his *Essay on the Picturesque, as Compared with the Sublime and the Beautiful*. Price was very much concerned with the gardening aspect of the picturesque debate, and much of his *Essay* is devoted to lambasting Capability Brown, safely dead so unable to answer back, though Repton, treated with more circumspection, was still around. Price's *Essay* is a polemic, emphatic in its pronouncements on the picturesque, which he distinguishes from the beautiful as the contrast between smoothness and roughness. Qualities of harmony and uniformity attributed to beauty, whereas the interest of the picturesque lies in its elements of surprise, irregularity: "A temple or palace of Grecian architecture in its perfect entire state, and with its surface and colour smooth and even, either in painting or reality is beautiful; in ruin it is picturesque. Observe the process by which time . . . converts a beautiful object into a picturesque one. First, by means of weather stains, partial incrustations, mosses, &c. it at the same time takes off from the uniformity of the surface, and of the colour; that is, gives it a degree of roughness, and variety of tint."

So, ruins good, pristine constructions bad. But Price extended his comparisons rather wildly to animals; where dogs were concerned a Pomeranian or rough water dog was picturesque, a smooth spaniel or greyhound not, a worn-out carthorse or wild forester was preferable to a "sleek pampered steed," goats superior to sheep, and a lion to a lioness (the mane, you see). And when it came to "our own species," beggars, gypsies and "all such rough tattered figures" were picturesque in the same way. One would like to think that he is writing tongue in cheek here, but I'm not at all sure that he is—the picturesque was an extremely serious matter for Price. Tom Stoppard's landscape gardener Mr. Noakes in *Arcadia* had certainly paid attention to him—one of the requirements of his proposed improvement of Sidley Park is the construction of a hermitage, to be occupied by a hermit. Lady Croom supposes that he will supply the hermit, and when he admits that he does not have one to hand, she is aghast:

LADY CROOM: Not one? I am speechless.

NOAKES: I am sure a hermit can be found. One could advertise.

LADY CROOM: Advertise?

NOAKES: In the newspapers.

LADY CROOM: But surely a hermit who takes a newspaper is not a hermit in whom one can have complete confidence.

Price is after variety, intricacy, the capacity to invite curiosity in the viewer: the picturesque "corrects the languor of beauty or the horror of sublimity." Fortunately, the sublime does not much arise in a landscape gardening context, so it is the correction of the merely beautiful that is at issue, beauty being "One cause of the insipidity that has prevailed under the name of improvement." And this is when he really gets going with his attack on Brown: "this great legislator of our national taste." He derides Brown's fixation with smooth sweeps of grass and groups and belts of trees: "the great distinguishing feature of modern improvement is the *clump*; whose name, if the first letter were taken away, would most accurately describe its form and effect." Brown's calm expanses of water won't do because they lack the element of reflection—the banks—of the overhanging trees and other growth that would supply interest: "I am aware that Mr Brown's admirers, with one voice, will quote the great water at Blenheim as a complete answer to all I have said against him on the subject . . ." He goes on to make specific criticism of the layout of the Blenheim lake and bridge. Years ago, when we lived a few miles away, I spent much time precisely there, sitting on the despised bank by the water, with not a thought about the nature of the picturesque, but fascinated by the courtship displays of the great crested grebe. Actually, applying Price criteria, I think a grebe would be more acceptably picturesque than, say, a mallard—that crest, a generally more edgy appearance.

"Mr Brown was bred a gardener," says Price dismissively, "and having nothing of the mind, or the eye of a painter, he formed his style (or rather his plan) upon the model of a parterre; and transferred its minute beauties, its little clumps, knots, and patches of flowers, the oval belt that surrounds it, and all its twists and crincum crancums, to the great scale of nature." And that is what is very much at issue: Price wants the natural effect. Brown, he says, is only satisfied when he has made a natural river look like an artificial one. He loathes Brown's use of clumps of firs or larches; he wants the kind of mixed woodland that provides variety of texture, of light and shade. On and on he goes, citing instances of Brownian abuse of the landscape on every page, ending up with a sigh: "It is equally probable that many an English gentleman has felt deep regret when Mr Brown had improved some charming trout stream into a piece of water; and that many a time afterwards, when walking along its naked banks, and disgusted with its glare and formality, he has thought how beautifully fringed those of his little brook once had been; how it sometimes ran rapidly over the stones and shallows, and sometimes in a narrower channel stole silently beneath the overhanging boughs."

I am afraid that Price got personal before he was done with Brown: "I have heard numberless instances of his arrogance and despotism, and such high pretensions seem to me little justified by his work. Arrogance and imperious manners, which, even joined to the truest merit and the most splendid talents, create disgust and opposition, when they are the off-spring of a little narrow mind, elated with temporary favour, provoke ridicule, and deserve to meet with it." And this swipe at the great Capability would have been widely read. Peacock certainly drew inspiration from the *Essay*, allowing his character Sir Patrick O'Prism to use a phrase of Price, at one point, when denigrating the use of "clumps," like "so many spots of ink, flicked at random out of a pen." Though the landscape architect in Headlong Hall is based rather more on Repton, who did indeed display an awareness of the picturesque, and is let off by Price with a mild remonstrance: "Mr Repton (who is deservedly at the head of his profession) might effectually correct the errors of his predecessors, if to his taste and facility in drawing . . . he was to add an attentive study of what the higher artists have done, both in their pictures and drawings." This leniency may have been a recognition that Repton was at least making some effort in the direction of the picturesque, or, perhaps, caution where someone still alive and vocal was concerned.

Jane Austen was certainly familiar with the concept of the picturesque. The matter is raised in *Northanger Abbey*, when Catherine Morland is walking near Bath with Henry Tilney, the young man she will eventually marry, and his sister: "The Tilneys were viewing the country with the eyes of persons accustomed to drawing, and decided on its capability of being formed into pictures, with all the eagerness of real taste . . . In the present instance [Catherine] confessed and lamented her want of knowledge; declared she would give any thing in the world to be able to draw; and a lecture on the picturesque immediately followed, in which his instructions were so clear that she soon began to see beauty in everything admired by him, and her attention was so earnest, that he became perfectly satisfied of her having a great deal of natural taste. He talked of fore-grounds, distances, and second distances—side-screens and perspectives—lights and shades;—and Catherine was so hopeful a scholar, that when they gained the top of Beechen Cliff, she voluntarily rejected the whole city of Bath, as unworthy to make part of a landscape."

These various publications—both descriptive and fictional—give a good idea of the intensity of discussion around the concept of the picturesque in the late eighteenth century. It all seems rather bizarre today—such passionate stances, the challenges to the discerning traveler, let alone to the fashionably inclined landowner—and the more so in that since then the word itself has quite lost its loaded quality. To describe something or somewhere today as picturesque has an almost pejorative connotation—there is a whiff of thatched cottages. The term has moved away from its implications of artistic perfection to a suggestion of mere charm, though with a hint of the contrived. And I'm not sure that anyone now would really want their garden called picturesque.

Today's stately home has to earn its keep, and the owner is probably more concerned with box-office appeal than anything else, for which a good garden may indeed be an asset, but cutting-edge fashion is less of a requirement than some remarkable feature, such as topiary yew hedges, spectacular water or intricate landscaping. And the same applies lower down the garden scale; at the time of writing, I have just made my first Yellow Book garden visit of the year, and came away not with a garden fashion suggestion but an entirely practical one—that a grouping of pot-grown tulips of different varieties looks just as fine if the pots are basic black plastic ones rather than fancy pots—such is the interest of the tulips that you somehow don't notice the pots. Indeed, fashion is not an issue for the Yellow Book, thanks be, which accounts for its range and its success: a display of every imaginable kind, size, shape and quality of garden.

When gardening fashionably you do not really consider that that is what you are doing, and probably it was always so, except where the wilder excesses of the eighteenth century were concerned. Any gardener is constricted by what is available, and what can be afforded. Availability depends on when and where you are gardening, and how you set about it will indeed be directed by the influences of the day—it will be fingered by Gertrude Jekyll or William Robinson or Vita Sackville-West or what was featured on *Gardeners' World* this week—but it never feels quite like that. It feels more like opportunity than fashion, so that having labeled this section as dealing with the fashionable garden, I find myself backing off; gardeners, I think, are opportunists, not slaves to fashion. Most know a good thing when they see one, and are flexible and pragmatic enough to change course if that looks expedient. I like to think that many a late-Victorian gardener would have heaved a sigh of relief at the suggestion that there was life beyond carpet bedding.

Time, Order and the Garden

To garden is to elide past, present and future; it is a defiance of time. You garden today for tomorrow; the garden mutates from season to season, always the same, but always different. In my vegetable gardening days, while digging a trench for the potatoes I would remember the Majestics I grew last year, and wonder how the Maris Pipers I am putting in today will compare. In autumn, I plant up a pot of "Tête-à-Tête" daffodils, seeing in the mind's eye what they will look like in February, and comparing them with "Hawera," which I found grew rather too tall last year. We are always gardening for a future; we are supposing, assuming, a future. I am doing that at eighty-three; the *Hydrangea paniculata* "Limelight" I have just put in will outlast me, in all probability, but I am requiring it to perform while I can still enjoy it.

The great defiance of time is our capacity to remember—the power of memory. Time streams away behind us, and beyond, but individual memory shapes, for each of us, a known place. We own a particular piece of time; I was there, then, I did this, saw that, felt thus. And gardening, in its small way, performs a memory feat: it corrals time, pinning it to the seasons, to the gardening year, by summoning up the garden in the past, the garden to come. A garden is never just *now*; it suggests yesterday, and tomorrow; it does not allow time its steady progress.

The garden—any garden—is in a state of unstoppable change. Each day, each week, each leaf, each bud, each flower—moving inexorably on to its next incarnation, the spring sparkle forgotten by the time of the summer show, that too fallen away before smoldering autumn. Then dead of winter, but one determined rose with a flower at Christmas.

I can't imagine living—gardening—somewhere with an unvarying climate. Well, I suppose I have lived thus, in fact: the Egyptian winter temperature is in the mid-sixties—you reached for a cardigan, at most. Summer, of course, soared to the nineties and beyond; the gardener's problem was water, water. Not an unvarying climate—a Mediterranean climate, I think—but one without recognizable seasons, except for hot summers and rather cooler winters. I know that when I came to England at the age of twelve I was aghast at the English winter: how did people endure this degree of cold? I had never before met the requisite garments: woolly jumpers, Chilprufe vests, a thick coat. Normal dress, in my experience, was a cotton frock, month in and month out. And where was the sun? When it appeared, it was a tepid affair, quite unrelated to Egypt's blistering globe.

I acclimatized, slowly, and have long since come to relish a properly seasonal climate: that reliable, progressive change, breeding lilacs out of the dead land, and everything else that it does. Made for gardeners, a temperate climate; appreciation is intensified, enjoyment heightened because you know the tulips won't be here for long, make the most of them, but, never mind, there is summer to come—roses, roses all the way. Our climate builds in that sense of gardening anticipation: it is the ever-rolling stream, sequential, cyclical, and meaning that there is never time to get tired of anything in the garden because it is always a temporary pleasure, and would we feel the same about the roses if they blazed on and on, in relentless flower, all of them hurtling through Christmas, instead of that one defiant unseasonal bloom? Several mild winters and the virtually frost-free climate of my London garden have meant that a large central pot of geraniums has now overwintered three times, turning themselves into perennials. They are on their fourth summer, and I am a bit tired of them.

Certainly, for me, part of the appeal of gardening is this ambivalent relationship with time; the garden performs in cycles, it reflects the seasons, but it also remembers and anticipates, and in so doing takes the gardener with it.

> Time present and time past
> Are both perhaps present in time future
> And time future contained in time past.

Did Eliot garden? The poem has sunflower, clematis, lotus, and "the moment in the rose-garden." Whether he did or not doesn't really matter—suffice it that whatever else "Burnt Norton" is about, to my mind it is about garden time.

Anticipation is central, where garden time is concerned. Gardening anticipation is an exaggerated form of the looking-forward element that we all reach for, cling on to, the beacon somewhere ahead, the promised day, the expected friend, lover, child, parent. With expectation to be savored meanwhile, the foretaste, the shadow, but with its own enticing pleasure.

Tulips, for me, right now in August. The tulips in the mind that I shall have in the garden next April and May. I have gone mad, run amuck, ordered seventy tulip bulbs, fired up by the canny example of a garden we visited this year that grew them packed close in large pots, the pots then grouped and clumped, and the effect was stunning. So I am appreciating twice over: now, and again then, when the tulips materialize: garden time. Oh, and the whole satisfying process of planting the bulbs; three bites of the cherry.

The garden reorders time. And to garden is to impose order. Any gardener does that, anywhere, requiring this to grow rather than the couch grass, the bindweed, the dandelion and the hairy bittercress that would do so otherwise; gardening is a manipulation of nature, the creation of an ordered state where nature would insist on disorder. It is the conquest of nature, the harnessing of nature to a purpose, initially practical, and later aesthetic.

In Willa Cather's *My Ántonia*, the pioneer families in Nebraska create gardens in the middle of the rolling red grass of the prairie, little islands of order amid the endless reach of the untouched landscape—big yellow pumpkins, rows of potatoes, and within a decade or so they have established orchards, cherry trees with gooseberry and currant bushes between the rows and a grape arbor with a seat. It is an extraordinary image—you can imagine the gardens, visualize them, so eloquent in what they say of pioneer life.

Of Willa Cather's twelve novels, I have always found *My Ántonia* the most powerful, and its strength lies in the images that it conjures up of pioneering life in the nineteenth century. She was drawing on her own experience; born in Virginia in 1873, she moved with her family when very young to Nebraska, to a place where, as she says in *My Ántonia*, "There was nothing but land: not a country at all but the material out of which countries are made." She had known early pioneers like the Shimerdas, Ántonia's family, living in sod houses, built of earth; writing of those like them she conjured up the whole history of the pouring of the old world into the new, the peasant societies of Europe, who, along with migrants from within America, opened up the West. They plowed up the prairie, and that symbolic plow lights up one of her most arresting passages: "The sun was sinking just behind it. Magnified across the distance by the horizontal light, it stood out against the sun, was exactly contained within the circle of the disk; the handles, the tongue, the share—black against the molten red. There it was, heroic in size, a picture writing on the sun." The Cather family moved soon from their first settlement into Red Cloud, the small prairie town where Willa spent her teenage years, and which she made into the fictional prairie town in *My Ántonia*, and today it is the center of the Willa Cather Foundation, a shrine to one of America's most significant writers.

A similar image crops up in Laura Ingalls Wilder's children's books about a pioneer family, *Little House on the Prairie*. "Every day they all looked at that garden. It was rough and grassy because it was made in the prairie sod, but all the tiny plants were growing. Little crumpled leaves of peas came up, and tiny spears of onions. The beans themselves popped out of the ground. But it was a little yellow bean-stem, coiled like a spring, that pushed them up. Then the bean was cracked open and dropped by two baby bean-leaves, and the leaves unfolded flat to the sunshine."

I remember reading that to my children in a hotel room somewhere in France, during a summer holiday trip, and we were all completely transported to another time, and another place. Laura Ingalls Wilder, like Willa Cather, had personal experience on which to draw. She was born in 1867 in the Big Woods area of Wisconsin, and the family moved from there to Kansas, and later to Minnesota and eventually Dakota. In all of these places they lived the pioneering life, and later, as a married woman, Laura led a farming life in Missouri, and began to write the series of books for children that were eventually to become a multimillion-dollar mass-marketing enterprise. Today there are Laura Ingalls Wilder museums in Missouri, Wisconsin, Minnesota, South Dakota, Iowa and Kansas, offering Laura Days, gift shops, memorabilia. She is an industry, effectively, but never mind—none of that can detract from the vitality of her work, narratives that so beautifully evoke an elsewhere, and the people who were there, books that no child should be without. Or adult; I read them still.

The pioneer garden was practical, essential, part of the whole grinding process of taming virgin territory for human use and habitation. In Europe, this had happened during what the archaeologists call the Neolithic revolution, the movement from hunter-gathering to farming, the deliberate planting of crops for harvesting that would mean that people could stay in one place. References to Neolithic *gardening* as such are hard to find (yes, I have tried), but there must have been points when farming shaded away into gardening, the establishment of little plots near the hut, the habitation, for those useful herbs and legumes, which would themselves sometimes shade from the purely utilitarian to the decorative. Some Neolithic habitation owner would have noticed a plant with an attractive flower: let's dig it up, and have it where we can see it. All right, pure fantasy, but Neolithic pottery is patterned, often elegantly so, there is Neolithic jewelry, clearly intended for personal adornment, all of which suggests an aesthetic sense, a need to go beyond mere necessity. I want to think of the first gardeners, back in the Stone Age, imposing order where order there was none, making a place that was pleasant to look at.

So, further powers of the garden: to refute time, to impose order. Both of which sound too grandiloquent; any garden is itself only tenuously in existence, it depends entirely on whoever is in charge of it. If neglected or abandoned, it will melt away before the onslaught of nettle, bramble and ivy, leaving only a memory stain in the form of those ancient Egyptian planting holes, or the surviving bony structure of hard landscaping in a later age. After my grandmother's death, that was what happened to her Somerset garden; her daughter, the artist Rachel Reckitt, had neither the time nor the urge to garden, and also had an ultra-environmentalist belief that any growth that has put itself somewhere should be allowed to remain. The hard landscaping survived—the rill, the sunken rose garden—but the flower beds dissolved under grass and much else, and saplings sprang up all over the place and were given occupational rights. In the kitchen garden, some long low grassy mounds remembered the asparagus beds, a few overgrown gooseberry bushes and the lines of unpruned espalier apple trees remained in determined but challenged production. It was a garden in retreat, proving the point that a garden is evanescent, it can fade in months, vanish in years.

In that sense, it would seem that time shoulders a garden aside, which is true enough, but the garden's power of defying time is something different—it is what the garden, the activity of gardening, does for you, me, for anyone. Gardening, you escape the tether of time, you experience that elision of past, present and future.

Time may obliterate a garden; it does not so much have its way with individual growths. When my grandmother laid out that garden, in around 1920, she planted a wisteria up the house. By the late 1940s, when I was spending all my school holidays there, it embraced two sides, poking its tendrils in at the windows, swamping them in blue when the flowers were out. By the time my aunt died, in 1998, and the house had to be sold, the thick gray limbs of the wisteria reached many yards away from the original stem, wrapping the house. So, a wisteria that was a good seventy years old. Probably not a record—apparently there is one on a cottage near Bridport in Dorset that is said to be a hundred—but the wisteria was the one tenacious element of the original garden planting. A subsequent owner had it hacked right back; I hope that its stem fights on.

There are numbers of long-lived garden plants. The rose is capable of hanging in there for decades, if unmolested. In our Oxfordshire garden there were two huge old shrub rose bushes (I never did manage to identify which they were), planted by the lady who had laid out the garden in about 1950, so around twenty-five years old. They were still flourishing when we left in 1998, so by then nearly fifty, and having received little or no attention except for an occasional attack on dead wood. The rhododendron is apparently about as tenacious as anything, can live for hundreds of years, and is so invasive that it will smother all other growth and create a rhododendron wilderness which can only be eradicated with heavy machinery. I have never cared for them, and, learning this, I think I understand why; along with being altogether too showy, there is something aggressive about them, a triffid-like quality. No, thank you.

Trees, of course, are another matter. In this country, we have the oak and the yew, both of which can live to a most respectable age. Yews in churchyards get to survive longest—sited there in the first place, it is claimed, because their longevity, and their evergreen status, are symbolic of Christ's transcendence of death. Top bidder for the record is the yew in the churchyard of St. Cynog's at Defynnog near Sennybridge in Wales, claiming 5,000 years, with the Fortingall Yew in the churchyard of that village as runner-up at 3,000. Impressive indeed, but the St. Cynog's claim would have it with a toe in the Neolithic and doing nicely in the Bronze Age, and thus long before implications of a Christian symbolism. Though many early churches are sited at a place which has previously had sacred significance. So maybe the yew had a more ancient connotation.

When it comes to the oak, chief contender seems to be the Bowthorpe Oak at Bourne in Lincolnshire, claiming 1,000 years and with a girth of forty feet. It looks stumpy in its Internet image—vast squat trunk sporting a crown of branches, not so much a majestic oak as one that has settled down and hung on grimly, surviving today in the orchard of a farm and yours to view for a £2.50 contribution to the Lincolnshire Air Ambulance. It is said to be in the Domesday Book. Really? It would have been an infant oak at the time, and I don't think Domesday listed trees anyway—indeed a cursory Domesday search finds no such mention. Far more suggestive is the thought that John Clare knew it. Clare, whose poems so celebrate the English countryside, was the son of a farm laborer, and lived at Helpston, not far from the oak. The poem in which he addresses it dates apparently from around the 1830s, and his words suggest that it looked much the same then as now:

> Solitude
> Paints not a lonelier picture to the view,
> Burthorp! than thy one melancholy tree,
> Age-rent, and shattered to a stump. Yet new
> Leaves come upon each rift and broken limb
> With every spring; and Poesy's visions swim
> Around it, of old days, and chivalry;
> And desolate fancies bid the eyes grow dim
> With feelings, that Earth's grandeur should decay,
> And all its olden memories pass away.

Elsewhere, it is the bristlecone pine, in California and Nevada, that lives longest, with the oldest tree in the world, aptly named Methuselah, in California's White Mountains, its exact location kept secret, and its age allegedly around

5,000 years. There are also clonal colonies which are very much older, where there are no individual trees of conspicuous age but the organism belowground that throws up new stems can be very old indeed—a colony of Huon pine trees in Tasmania around 10,000, and a colony of quaking aspens in Utah estimated at 80,000.

For me, that doesn't have the same impact; I want the visible surviving tree with an accredited age. And I wonder why it is that an ancient tree is somehow more emotive than an ancient building? John Clare evidently responded in that way to the Bowthorpe Oak, with Poesy's visions and so forth; I think it is to do with the feeling that a tree is in some way sentient, which a building is not. Anthropomorphism, but it certainly has that effect on me. The thought that that oak presided over the labors of medieval peasants, sat out the Civil War and the enclosure movement and the Industrial Revolution . . . That that Welsh yew was seen by someone in the Bronze Age . . . Buildings do not have the same charge, for me. I have lived the last forty years of my life in old houses, moving from 1530 to 1620 to relatively modern 1833, and while I respected (and respect) their longevity and the fact that I am just one of many passing through them, my predecessors are never conjured up in the same way, or the thought that the house has seen and experienced like a tree. Which the tree did not; pure animism, and absurd, but there it is.

I have never gone in for tree-hugging, but I can feel a certain empathy with the activity. My own animistic tendency where trees are concerned certainly began in childhood, back in that Egyptian garden where I communed regularly with a particular eucalyptus tree. But in our neighbors' garden there was a banyan tree, of which I was deeply envious, certain that they valued it less than I did; it should have been in our garden. The banyan is a kind of fig—not that you would ever suspect that—and is sometimes called the "strangler fig" on account of its growth habit. Banyan seeds are dispersed by birds, and when one lands on the trunk or branch of a tree (or a building), it will send roots downward, and may "strangle" the host structure. This effect can be seen on abandoned ancient sites in India or Cambodia. Our neighbors' banyan was an old tree, and as such it had aerial prop roots hanging down from its branches—long tough rope-like roots strong enough for a child to swing on, many of these, so that the tree covered a large area, with a main trunk of clustered roots, and others swaying free. The grown-ups used it as a shady sitting place, we children swung from the roots, or tied two together to make a seat. A most satisfactory tree. The banyan is the national tree of India, and is considered sacred; in many villages a banyan will be the centerpiece, a shady place for gossip or commerce, and, I hope, for children to enjoy.

In old age, you think of yourself as time made manifest: this body, with which time has had its way, undergoing metamorphosis from decade to decade, fetching up, it seems, as someone else. Trees do it rather more expressively, recording their own age with neat precision. Tree rings are wonderfully eloquent; here is time stated, time recorded, time made manifest. Dendrochronology—the scientific method of dating based on the analysis of tree rings—can determine past climates, or the age of a building, it can be used to calibrate radiocarbon dating, or by art historians to determine the date of a panel painting. And all because a tree grows slowly, systematically, but laying down each year a memory of what that year was like—unusually wet, dry, cold, hot—whether the tree flourished and grew, or held back, and how many years have passed. And, the more I think about it, the more I have to come to the conclusion that this is why trees invite anthropomorphism. They *are* sentient, in a way that a building cannot be.

Any garden is a defined area, within which the gardener attempts to impose order. The garden resists, and defies the imposition by throwing up docks, couch grass, bind-weed and anything else that occurs to it at any spot the gardener has not been watching intently. I have been infected by Karel Čapek here, I see—but it does, it does, as any gardener knows. More than that, it does not observe its own boundaries. Walking the lane beside Josephine's Somerset garden this spring, I saw that her euphorbia had nipped through the hedge and joined the red campion, the stitch-wort, the primroses on the hedge bank. The primrose, incidentally, is the West Somerset weed; the lanes in spring have cliffs of primrose, walls of primrose, carpets of prim-rose. In the garden they have to be sternly treated—culled, moved elsewhere.

Escaping euphorbia. Garden escapes—I rather love them. Red valerian, in Somerset, springing from every wall; it especially favors walls. Clumps of blue anchusa. Valerian is a native of the Mediterranean area, but its escaping ten-dency means that it has naturalized all over the globe: the

United States, Australia, and is a most firmly settled immigrant in this country. Anchusa is native to Europe, and parts of Africa and Asia, and evidently considers itself so here, though there are of course many different garden species. Buddleia . . . *Buddleia davidii* came here from China in the 1890s, got dug in as a garden plant, and soon made its way out of the garden and into any waste ground it could find. In its natural habitat it prefers stony soil, and therefore pounced on the rough ballast along the edge of railway lines, thus fanning out all over the country. Ragwort, incidentally, did just the same thing—Oxford ragwort, jumping out of Oxford's Botanic Garden, achieving the railway station in the early nineteenth century and setting off from there along the Great Western Railway and eventually all over the country. Buddleia is the butterfly bush, and so is valuable in that sense. We had a huge white buddleia in the Oxfordshire garden and in a good butterfly year there would be clouds of them around it—Painted Ladies, Peacocks, Red Admirals, Cabbage Whites, Brimstones, Clouded Yellows, Commas, everything. In London, it is the urban opportunist, particularly enjoying a good roof site; where I am, many roofs sprout a whiskery fringe of buddleia in a gutter. The escapist is invariably the pale lilac one; plenty of more interesting varieties to be had for the garden—the deep purple one is my choice, or the white.

Soon after I came to England in 1945, at age twelve, I was taken by a family friend to the area around St. Paul's, in London. He wanted to show me how the bombing had revealed the original Roman walls of the city. But what I remember most vividly is the sea of purple in every bomb site, acres of purple on every side, occupying what had been the basements of bombed buildings: rosebay willowherb, fireweed—bombweed, as it came to be called. *Chamaenerion angustifolium* was actually considered to be a garden plant until the mid eighteenth century, when it set about colonizing the wild. I doubt if any gardener cultivates it now, though Jack and I mistakenly did so, in our first garden in Swansea, planting out a whole lot of neat little green rosettes that we thought must be something to be cherished. Willowherb seems to have escaped from the garden long ago; it flourishes in poor soil and waste places, and, like buddleia, proceeded along the railway lines. And it relished a place where there has been fire—hence its colonization of bombed London.

And there are other "historic" garden escapes that have gone native and are still valued in the garden. *Fuchsia magellanica* arrived from South America as a garden shrub, and can now be found as naturalized hedging, especially in Ireland, the Isle of Man, and in Devon. The fritillary, that most elegant of all the spring bulbs, with its drooping checkered heads, dusky purple or white, seems to be mysterious in origin, not recorded in the wild until the early eighteenth century, and so seen as possibly an escape from Tudor gardens. It is elusive enough to be considered as something of a rarity in the wild, and has been brought back into the garden by the discriminating gardener. Honesty—*Lunaria annua*—grown as a garden plant as much for its transparent silvery seed-pods, treasured by the flower arranger, as for its purple flowers, came originally from southeast Europe, but has left the garden and naturalized on waste and on roadsides. The rhododendron can be a pest where it has ousted everything else and made dense thickets. More welcome is little ivy-leafed toadflax, that engaging thing that swarms over walls and banks, finds its way into garden steps—a seventeenth-century introduction used in gardens then but now gone wild entirely. And there are many other escapers that began here in cultivation and have jumped the wall: the laburnum, Russell lupins, stag's horn sumach, the snapdragon. And, definitely, my beloved *Erigeron karvinskianus*, its sparkling daisy flowers lighting up railings and basements all around my patch of London, as I write, in late June.

You can't impose order, where nature is concerned. A garden may be a defined area, but it is also an artificial concept, and plants will evade definition if it suits them—jump the wall and flourish elsewhere. It seems a form of give-and-take: the garden colonizes the wild, the wild probes the garden, sending up natural growth wherever it gets the chance. What is a weed, and what is not? Jack and I used to have the occasional stand-off over vetch, both bush vetch and tufted vetch, which I thought too appealing to be always rooted out, and which he classified as weed. Equally, toadflax—so pretty, that pale primrose yellow. Not so, in his view. Same issue as a daisy-sprinkled lawn.

Actually, the distinction between garden plant and wild one seems arbitrary. Take cow parsley; if it were a rarity, rather than the stuff that so gloriously foams along the roads and lanes in June, we would be buying it at garden centers and cosseting it. Similarly red campion; if there were not drifts of it every year, so ubiquitous that you cease to notice it, Monty Don would be advocating it on *Gardeners' World*. We grow morning glory—an annual—for its cerulean blue, and because it is a reminder of the Mediterranean, swarming there over everyone's balcony or terrace; we wage war on bindweed, that most tenacious and ineradicable perennial "weed," but actually, to look at, convolvulus is just a small white form of morning glory, and, if annual and more genteel in behavior, we would probably cherish it.

In fact, a skillful gardener/botanist could create a show garden comprised entirely of so-called "weeds"; now there's an idea for Chelsea.

The imposition of order, in the garden, is the requirement that things grow where you want them to do so, rather than behaving naturally and putting themselves just anywhere. You persuade them too by providing the circumstances that they prefer, just the right amount of sun, shade, damp or dry, by pampering with compost, bone meal, fertilizer, whatever. You fool the plant into thinking this is exactly where it chose to be: anthropomorphism again—I know, I know—but that is what gardening can make you feel you are up against. The weeds, of course, are another matter, a different anthropomorphic thinking: an extermination of the proletariat, a bout of ethnic cleansing. Gardening induces a polarized vision of the plant world, when it comes to this pursuit of an ordered space.

And the space itself is an imposition, an artificial creation. Hard landscaping, we call it today, a process that has gone on for thousands of years, worldwide, from Babylon and Pompeii, through the Taj Mahal and the Alhambra and the Villa d'Este and Versailles and the excavations of Capability Brown down to the personal endeavors of today's back garden: the paved patio, the gravel path, the water feature, the hedge, the fence, the wall. All of them with one purpose: the imposition of order where nature rejects order, the creation of an ordered space that is also an aesthetic endeavor—artistry with earth, wood, stone, and everything that grows.

I remember flying into Los Angeles once and seeing spread out below, as the plane descended, a great acreage of small enclosures each with its rectangle of blue: the swimming pool. The Californian equivalent of a water feature, I suppose; quite a challenge to landscape effectively, and indeed I don't remember ever hearing of a Chelsea show garden that offered one—rather the rill, the cascade, the environmentally friendly reed-fringed pond. Though, that said, I have seen various Chelsea gardens with—to my mind—constructions as uncomfortable in a garden context as a swimming pool: sheet metal slabs, graceless pieces of sculpture, blocks of concrete. Well, taste is an eclectic matter, and the ordering of space in terms of gardening is a nice demonstration of the vicissitudes of taste, from the Babylon flight of fancy—hanging trees up in the air—to the geometric formalities of André Le Nôtre in the seventeenth century, which seem like order carried to obsession.

But, never mind taste, what is so intriguing for any garden lover is that there is no end to the possibilities offered by this ordering of space. We have just visited the Piet Oudolf garden at Durslade Farm in Somerset, and, for me, every conventional assumption about a garden was over-turned. Here is an entirely innovative interpretation of order: a garden that is a group of large areas—you can't quite call them beds—that are closely planted, with wide paths in which to wander between them. The whole place is a sequence of billowing color masses, mounds of color interspersed with moments of height and structure. A pal-ette of purples, blues, soft mauves, splashed here and there with yellow, orange, light green—a symphony of colors. Repeat planting of, apparently, 115 different plants, gives harmony; everywhere there are clumps of waving grasses, foaming grasses, taller and stiffer grass, here a sweep of creamy yellow achillea, there a patch of purple sedum alongside clumps of light green prairie grass, a burst of blue salvia, a stand of orange helenium or steel-blue echinops. There is contrast of height, of texture, of color above all, but always this sense of the billowing masses of plants, of the color mounds that are expertly ordered but appear some-how entirely natural. We loved it—enthralled by the concept, and puzzled by unfamiliar growths. With good reason, I later discover, studying the plan with its key to plantings: *Filipendula rubra* "Venusta"? *Sanguisorba* "Red Button"? *Eupatorium maculatum* "Atropurpureum"? *Molinia caerulea*? This was innovative gardening in a class of its own—the gardening of the future, perhaps. Though only for some; you need space for this, the generous space in which to create order.

The Jekyll/Robinson concept of contrived disorder still dominates today, the idea of basic structure overlaid by the natural performance of a planting scheme—entirely

satisfying when skillfully carried out, with its sense of subtle manipulation, plants persuaded to enhance, establish an
artificial design. A Lutyens-style flight of stone steps, lined
with *Erigeron karvinskianus*; a Robinsonian grass walk, bordered with drifts of narcissi.

In the vegetable garden, order is necessity: drifts of carrot
won't do. You regiment your peas and beans: straight lines,
no crowding. Also deeply satisfying, in a different way—
nicely marshaled rows of well-behaved veg, doing what
they are supposed to do and no nonsense about aesthetic
effect. Which will arrive anyway: the scarlet flowers of runner beans swarming up their poles, the color contrasts of
lettuce—red "Lollo Rossa" among the greens. You regiment, you discipline, you require good order, you practice
crop rotation. Disorder will of course lurk, always: the
opportunist weeds, the slug, the snail, the caterpillar. Out
with the hoe; in with some ethnic cleansing. The mollusk
and arthropod onslaught has to be endured, to some extent.
You pick them off, squash. The vegetable garden is hand-
managed, like the earliest farming, from which I suppose it
is descended.

And here in West Somerset, in mid-August, I see the ultimate form of gardening: farming today. The landscape is
ordered from end to end, the fields an array of geometric
yellow-gold shapes sectioned off by the dark green lines of
hedges. I have always been fascinated by landscape history,
so I know that the shapes are eloquent also: they tell of early
clearance, of changing usages, of the enclosure movement.
An excerpt from Ursula Fanthorpe's poem "Seven Types of
Shadow" is an elegant expression of this:

After a hot summer, fields grow talkative.
Wheat speaks in crop marks, grasses in parch marks.

Wheat or grass, what they tell is the truth
Of things that lay underneath five thousand years ago,

The forts, the barrows, the barns, the shrines, the walls.
These are the native ghosts. After a hot summer.

No haunting. No rattle of chains. They just lie there
In their rigid truthfulness, the ghosts of things.

I tramped around looking for all that, long ago. Deserted medieval villages a specialty; it was a triumph to locate one of those—the lumps and bumps of the buildings, the ridge and furrow of the once-fields. But now, above all—with my head at the moment full of gardening images—the shapes are the imposition of order, over hundreds of years, the subjection of a place that is programmed to run wild, to display the survival of the fittest. Walking Somerset lanes just now, the deep lanes with high hedge banks that are cliffs of primroses and ferns in spring but have now been sternly shorn back by Somerset County Council, I see on all sides the russet-tipped soft green of fresh oak leaves springing from the banks. This is oak country; left to itself, untouched by human hand, it would become a sea of oak, as I imagine it once was. Gardened for hundreds, thousands, of years, its oaks are restrained, kept in their place along the roadsides. Gardening as industry. And harvesting has just begun, so I am reminded that the implements required are on a

somewhat different scale from the hoe and the wheelbarrow; a combine harvester approaches, and there is not room
for me and it in the lane. I must either squeeze myself into
the bank, at my peril, or walk briskly ahead until we reach
a passing place, to the operator's irritation, no doubt.

I suppose that my addiction to television documentaries
on wild landscapes stems from some arcane need for, or
curiosity about, an untouched world, before humanity
stepped in and plowed it up. Yellowstone National Park in
the United States has been shown lately, at length, dramatic
in its geothermal features, its lakes and mountains, for one
used to the more tranquil landscape of England (tamed or
not), but nicely illustrative of a primeval landscape. Similarly the Australian bush, tracts of Africa. The world before
industrial gardening. I try to conjure up West Somerset
before we had our way with it—a world of oak, ash and
thorn, with nothing familiar except the contours that I
know today: the rise of the Brendons over there, Tre-
borough Common, our local high points—Dumbledeer,
Withycombe Common, Croydon Hill. And then another
combine harvester roars past, reality on the move.

> What wondrous life is this I lead!
> Ripe apples drop about my head;
> The luscious clusters of the vine
> Upon my mouth do crush their wine;
> The nectarine and curious peach
> Into my hands themselves do reach;
> Stumbling on melons as I pass,
> Insnared by flowers I fall on grass.

Meanwhile the mind, from pleasure less,
Withdraws into its happiness:
The mind, that ocean where each kind
Does straight its own resemblance find;
Yet it creates, transcending these,
Far other worlds, and other seas;
Annihilating all that's made
To a green thought in a green shade.

A book that is a reflection on gardens and gardening has to pay tribute to the green thought in the green shade, to that gardening poem that everyone knows. Marvell's metaphysical garden is a distinctly high-class place: apples, vine, nectarine, peach, melons, a fountain. Few seventeenth-century gardens would have risen to all that, and not many today, but that is neither here nor there; the point made is an abstract one, and any garden can apply. This is the garden as solace, the significance of a garden, of plants, of nature, as therapy. I'll buy that. Here's another way in which the garden defies time, gives order to the mind, the thoughts. The place of escape, of release from demands, requirements, obligations.

The form of the solace, therapy, will differ from person to person, gardener to gardener. For me, it has never so much been sitting about with the green thoughts but just being out there, probably doing something—sit about, and you at once spot some job that needs doing. But, at its most basic, it is simply that engagement with an impervious world; nature, I suppose you have to call it. Out there this morning, with some watering to be done, and dead-heading, and a pot or two to be moved around, I am joined immediately by the robin. It always appears, more or less at once. I do what I do, and it moves briskly about, one beady eye cocked in my direction. I am seen, I suppose, as some kind of ambulant tree, possibly a threat and therefore requiring close observation, but also useful because my activities invariably stir up insects. I like the robin, a lot; its presence lifts my spirits— that sharp black eye, its precise, purposeful hopping hither and thither. The robin doesn't *like* me—let's not get anthropomorphic—but I am an opportunity, to be seized. Whatever, we are in some kind of symbiosis. That is the therapy, the green thought, that the garden has served up. At other times, it is all the usual garden gifts: smells—a rose, a pinch of thyme, rosemary, artemisia, choisya; the turning of the year—the first green gleam of bulbs coming up, the hellebores out, roses with new growth, the acer's spring glow. There is a mindless satisfaction in all this; out there, looking, noticing, other concerns are temporarily shelved. Therapy.

In fact, the idea of the therapeutic garden is very much in the public domain, an accepted element in the treatment of health problems of one kind and another. There are elaborate, carefully designed therapeutic gardens attached to hospitals, hospices, medical centers, retirement communities, especially, it seems, in the United States, where the design of such gardens has become an art form. It is claimed that access to nature balances the circadian rhythms, lowers blood pressure, supplies vitamin D. I find circadian rhythms hard to understand; all organisms are subject to them, it seems—they tell plants when to flower—and for us humans the essential aspect is their direction of our sleeping and waking pattern. I don't see what the garden is doing here, I must say; vitamin D and the effect on blood pressure make perfect sense. In fact, it is this last that seems to me the crux of the matter; the garden and all that is therein can have a calming effect, which is exactly what Marvell was on about, rather more elegantly. For me, a ten-minute engagement with the robin—and the dead-heading, and the watering— puts out of my head a tiresome decision to be made, chores to be done, that nagging worry; it puts into the robin various ants, and a couple of small worms (I saw). Never mind the circadian rhythms, for either of us—the garden has provided. Sustenance for the robin, green thoughts for me, or rather, a therapeutic absence of thought.

I suppose that parks and open spaces are public therapy, municipal therapy. Hyde Park, Green Park, Central Park on the other side of the Atlantic: the great green lungs that every city needs, and that most have, acknowledgment by the state that people need space that is green and open. The need for green . . . I am constantly aware, and gratified, that London is a city of trees. Many of them the London plane— *Platanus* × *acerifolia*—that splendid robust tree, apparently impervious to pollution, many decades old in some of the central squares (the ones in Berkeley Square possibly over 200 years), with those handsome trunks and the trademark black bobble seed heads in winter. The planes predominate, for good reason, but every London road, great and small, has trees. A few minutes' walk from my door there are several fine sorbus, a couple of eucalyptus, and within sight of my windows a laburnum, a chestnut, three different kinds of flowering cherry.

I am lucky to live on a London garden square, not one of those snobby gated Kensington ones that are for residents only, but one owned by the local authority, accessible to all. And much used—mothers with toddlers, office workers with a lunchtime sandwich. There are always a few people out there, sitting on the seats or the grass. Admittedly, rather too many a few years ago, when a teenage gang laid claim to the gardens (the only local space not "owned" by rival gangs, they told the police); much undesirable activity then, but by the next year the gang had found a better pitch, or grown up, and all was tranquil again. The square is lush with trees, has good grass spaces, rose beds where the planting is sensibly robust, much "Peace" and "Queen Elizabeth"—they have to take an occasional pasting from footballs.

Sometimes a lady takes a Pilates class out there, doing wonders for their circadian rhythms, I expect. People read there, sunbathe, picnic, rock a baby to sleep, stare at a mobile phone. There is plenty of bird life, and three rather stout semi-feral cats, who are fed by a local resident, but apparently not permitted house space. The gardens provide an oasis of green, and calm, in a bustling part of London.

The garden is therapeutic, but it seems to be a mantra now that gardening itself fosters the health. It is claimed that gardeners can live for up to fourteen years longer. Why? Because of all that vitamin D, and the exercise, but also because of getting the hands into the soil—exposure to natural bacteria boosts the immune system. On the exercise side, two hours of energetic gardening apparently uses up the same energy as a half-marathon of thirteen miles. And even the pottering kind of gardening done by the likes of me is strongly recommended; for older people, activity on a daily basis reduces the risk of stroke or heart attack by 27 percent, according to one study. And, indeed, a government health adviser said in 2015 that GPs should prescribe gardening to prevent the onset of dementia. Well, there are said to be six million active gardeners in Britain, so we can take heart, smugly confident that what we want to be doing anyway is also beneficial.

Someone said to me recently that getting keen on gardening had changed her life—a remark that would have interested me from anyone, but especially so in her case because she was young—around thirty. It confirmed my impression that the taste for gardening is getting younger—no longer the preserve of the middle-aged and beyond. Many lives being subtly changed . . . And what is it, this change?

I think it is all to do with the question of time, order—and perception. The assumption of a gardening persona gives you, me, anyone, that enriching lift out of the restrictions of now, and today. The gardener floats free of the present, and looks forward, acquires expectations, carries next spring in the mind's eye. And remembers, also, looks back, and considers then as compared with now, and next year. A gardener is able to see incipient promise everywhere: these nondescript stems and leaves will burst out into the creamy pink flowers of *Hydrangea* "Early Sensation," from this patch of bare earth will rise a clump of cerulean-blue grape hyacinths, come April, this dormant green shrub is going to light up spring with the rich red new leaves of *Pieris japonica* "Mountain Fire." Gardeners are dealt a rich store of anticipation.

And then there is the imposition of order. The gardener

has an objective: the weeding of that bed, the pruning of those roses, the digging of a potato trench. Nothing more salutary than a task satisfactorily completed. Cleaning a room or doing the washing up come nowhere near it; the garden job well done is visual pleasure, you can see and savor the effect of what you have done. Where there was an unsightly tangle there is a display of what should be there, instead of what should not; the roses stand neatly prepared for next year's growth; the trench awaits those seed potatoes. Gardening is not outdoor housework; it is a manipulation of the natural world, the creation of order where order is appropriate, the subtle adjustments of disorder where that would be effective. It is creative, in short.

Finally, the question of perception. I shall annoy non-gardener readers (should there be any) by saying that gardeners are more perceptive. Gardening, you look at how plants grow, you learn how different plants behave, you see the whole interactive process of soil, root, stem, flower, insect. You are up close and personal with nature. I remember a three-year-old granddaughter, given a trowel to keep her quiet while her mother gardened alongside, turning up a worm and gazing in utter fascination: earth had a new significance. I am always distracted by bees—the license you have to observe them closely, as they rummage inside a flower, laden with pollen, purposeful, intent. I can no longer get down on my knees, which is where a gardener needs to be, and I miss that intimacy with the ground, the close engagement with root structures, the proper division and replanting of an iris rhizome, the sowing of seeds.

Once a gardener, you look around you differently; you

notice more, you pay attention to the mundane, and you pounce at once on anything unfamiliar. Every gardener is an automatic taxonomist: the naming of things is essential, a plant you don't know is a challenge. What is that? Today, I photographed (furtively) a nearby window box; there was what looked like a dwarf Michaelmas daisy and you don't reckon to put Michaelmas daisies in window boxes; but, yes, it seems that there is one that is obligingly small—*Aster* "Dwarf Queen," I think. The gardener ends up with a head crammed full of names; I have the universal old-age failing with names and have to fish around now, but I have not yet stared at a rose wondering what kind of flower this is, and in fact plant names seem to surface more readily than those of politicians or celebrities, which is as it should be, as far as I'm concerned.

Gardening, we step beyond the dictation of time. We create order. We design and direct. We get right in there with the plants, escape worldly worries, do in our knees and our backs, set spinning our circadian rhythms, jack up our immune systems, and possibly live a few years longer. When hard at it, none of this is relevant; it is simply a matter of intense engagement with cutting back, taking out, putting in, with this rose, that weed, these seeds, bulbs, tubers. As an occupation, it seems to me unparalleled; productive, beneficial, enjoyable. What more could you want?

Style and the Garden

Gardening style is a social indicator. Eleanor Perényi noted this in *Green Thoughts*, recalling the discussion of U and non-U (upper class and non-upper class) prompted by the professor of linguistics at the University of Birmingham in 1954, and taken up by Nancy Mitford in an essay in *Encounter*. Speech was the matter at issue—whether you said napkin or serviette, what or pardon, drawing room or lounge, but Perényi extended it to flowers, observing that while, in Mitford's terms, everything transatlantic would be considered non-U, certain plants are definitely non-U either side of the Atlantic: gladioli, scarlet salvias, wax begonias, red-hot pokers, orange marigolds. Wax begonias, incidentally, are those small ones with thick waxy leaves, dark green or purple-brown, and clusters of pink, white or red flowers, often used as bedding plants. And here I put my hand up, defiantly. I have some white ones this summer, sharing a huge shallow pot with white impatiens, acquired at a garden center because the combination looked a good idea, and it is.

Nancy Mitford did not mention plants, focusing entirely on language, but she was clearly aware of the garden as social indicator. In her *The Pursuit of Love* (1945), young Linda, the offspring of aristocratic landed gentry, as U as you can get, makes an unwise marriage to the son of Sir

Leicester Kroesig, a *nouveau riche* banker. The Kroesig country house is in Surrey, which is of course not the shires, not real country at all:

> The garden which lay around it would be a lady water-colourist's heaven, herbaceous borders, rockeries, and water-gardens were carried to a perfection of vulgarity, and flaunted a riot of huge and hideous flowers, each individual bloom appearing twice as large, three times as brilliant as it ought to have been and if possible of a different colour from that which nature intended. It would be hard to say whether it was more frightful, more like glorious Technicolor, in spring, in summer, or in autumn. Only in the depth of winter, covered by the kindly snow, did it melt into the landscape and become tolerable.

Spring brings out the very worst:

> You could hardly see any beautiful, pale, bright, yellow-green of spring, every tree appeared to be entirely covered with a waving mass of pink or mauve tissue-paper. The daffodils were so thick on the ground that they too obscured the green, they were new varieties of a terrifying size, either dead white or dark yellow, thick and fleshy; they did not look at all like the fragile friends of one's childhood.

I think I recognize those daffodils: they sound like "King Alfred," that largest and most strident of all, beloved of parks and other municipal planting.

Perényi blames the hybridists for the introduction of

"unheard-of vulgarities to the garden world"—the creation of double this and that, larger and larger blooms, and indeed this condemnation ties in nicely with Vita Sackville-West's taste for all the small, single, discreet and unshowy varieties. Bold and brash was definitely *déclassé*.

In Angus Wilson's *The Middle Age of Mrs Eliot* (1958), Gordon and David are a gay couple who run a nursery garden. Not a garden center—those were not around yet, and, if they had been, would have been considered vulgar, populist, as compared with a proper nursery, which grew most of its own stuff. And still does—plenty exist today. Gordon and David are themselves connoisseurs of good-taste gardening, but commercial necessity obliges them to cater for a wide spectrum of customers:

> Azaleas and rhododendrons for the richer soil of the expense-account, weekend gentry who were their neighbours in the Forest to the north; delphiniums, dahlias, the most ordinary regular annuals for the "new poor" ladies below the chalk line to the south, from cottage gardens in the Downs to sad, windswept gardens without hope in the seaside refuges of the retired. And shrub roses for the more sophisticated—the rich "resting" stage stars, the lady novelists, and the local friends of Glyndebourne. It was a triumph of practicality over self-indulgence, David reflected.

Ah, shrub roses and lady novelists. Yes, all right, I have had shrub roses. Definitely the rose of choice for the discriminating gardener in the mid and late twentieth century. And the rose can indeed be said to be a socially indicating plant;

more on that in due course. Angus Wilson's couple had a small private garden tucked away beyond the nursery:

> At the moment iris reticulata gleamed purple and gold here and there in the sunshine, and a great mass of mauve iris stylosa still basked in the dusty, rubble-filled soil by the wall. Next there would be knots of crocus, daffodils and fritillary edging the lawn—in what Gordon had called "our very pleasing, vulgar little spring show." Later the beds were massed with tulips and later still with lilies. There were rose beds with hybrid tea and floribunda—for they were no rose specialists—but in Gordon's words "never a chic shrub rose."

There, the shrub rose is used to give Gordon and David a gardening taste that is so refined that it steps aside from the gardening practice of those who are just ordinarily discriminating. And there is another significant point: the reference to *Iris stylosa* and "dusty, rubble-filled soil" tells me that Angus Wilson was a gardener himself. To know that *Iris stylosa* requires that kind of site is quite an arcane piece of gardening knowledge and I don't think he would have written that had he not, in all probability, grown that iris himself at some point, somewhere. All novelists move on to dangerous territory when they devise a character with a background unfamiliar to them. Most do it and have to rely on research and inquiry, knowing that any slip-up will provoke comment from some sharp-eyed reader. But sometimes what looks to be natural accuracy is a giveaway too: I feel sure that Angus Wilson gardened.

We are in snob country here, of course. I find myself not all that keen on Gordon and David with their patronage of—effectively—all gardeners who are not them. And Nancy Mitford's *The Pursuit of Love* is a positive study of snobbery; she was the arch connoisseur and practitioner. Any discussion of social indicators invites the snobbery challenge, and this whole section has to take on that risk, but this is too intriguing an aspect of gardens, and gardening, to be ignored. We garden differently according to who we are. Karel Čapek was making that point, in his pre-war Czech way, when he distinguished between the window boxes of the rich and the poor. It would have been interesting to learn what, later, a totalitarian window box looked like.

I live in a part of London that has jumped, in seventy years or so, from working class/lower-middle class to distinctly affluent. Window boxes abound, and I would guess always have done, but there is no one now to tell me what the window box of the 1950s was like. Today's are various; this morning I noted that more people plump for the geranium than for anything else, with some forays into petunias, fuchsias, trailing begonias (my own, disregarding Monty Don's recent condemnation of these on *Gardeners' World*), and some fastidious departures by way of neat balls of box hedging, a delectable planting of blue pansies in a silver-gray metal window box, an elegant combination of white petunias and bacopa. By their windows ye shall know them.

Now, where is *this* garden?

People had always been told that the house at Skuytercliff was an Italian villa. Those who had never been to Italy believed it; so did some who had. The house had been built by Mr van der Luyden in his youth, on his return from the "grand tour," and in anticipation of his approaching marriage with Miss Louisa Dagonet. It was a large square wooden structure, with tongued and grooved walls painted pale green and white, a Corinthian portico, and fluted pilasters between the windows. From the high ground on which it stood a series of terraces bordered by balustrades and urns descended in the steel-engraving style to a small irregular lake with an asphalt edge overhung by rare weeping conifers. To the right and left, the famous weedless lawns studded with "specimen" trees (each of a different variety) rolled away to long ranges of grass crested with elaborate cast-iron ornaments; and below, in a hollow, lay the four-roomed stone house which the first Patroon had built on the land granted him in 1612.

Clearly, this is socially elevated gardening, snob gardening. And, indeed, it is the epitome of that: the garden of the Van der Luydens, in Edith Wharton's *The Age of Innocence*, who are the very apex of New York society in the late nineteenth century, a couple so strangled by ancestral glory as to be almost incapable of spontaneous speech. The central figure, Newland Archer, is a young man who married a girl from within that closed community of the wealthy and socially hidebound, but falls in love with Ellen Olenska, a woman who is of the "tribe" but has returned from Europe after having left a philandering Polish husband, and so is regarded as tainted and suspect. The story turns on the subtle and successful maneuvers of the families concerned to force Ellen back to Europe and out of Newland's life.

The description of the garden precedes one of the few, intense scenes between the lovers; Ellen is spending the weekend at the van der Luydens, during the period of her acceptance in polite society, and Newland visits her. The garden is there as further background to the lifestyle of these hugely prosperous and entirely self-absorbed families: power gardening, statement gardening. And the subtext of the novel is a scalding indictment of the rigid attitudes and requirements of that society. There is a parallel account later of a further garden, pertaining to another of the families: "The turf was hemmed with an edge of scarlet geranium and coleus, and cast-iron vases painted in chocolate color, standing at intervals along the winding path that led to the sea, looped their garlands of petunia and ivy geranium above the neatly raked gravel." Cast-iron ornaments seem to have been *de rigueur*, and the scarlet geranium and coleus combination has me shuddering.

I think Edith Wharton would have shuddered too, in real life, because the interesting thing is that she herself was a passionate gardener, or rather, creator of gardens. Wealthy, ferociously energetic, she created four gardens: one in Massachusetts and three in France, where she spent most of her life. She was knowledgeable, had written a book on Italian villas and their gardens, and was familiar with the works of Jekyll and Robinson. Her French gardens sound delectable, one at Saint-Brice, in the Île-de-France, with box-hedged parterres, a woodland space, a pond with fountain, a potager, an orchard, rose garden and blue garden, an avenue of lilies. This is lavish gardening, no-expense-spared gardening, but a far cry from the stifled garden style of that New York society she wrote about so eloquently. And, indeed, Hermione Lee, her biographer, has pointed out that in the seventeen years she spent at Saint-Brice, and at Sainte-Claire in the south of

France—another major operation and elaborate design—she made no fictional use of these experiences: her fictional gardens are precise, accurate, and are there as ballast to the narrative; her own gardening life was a world apart.

Yellow Book garden visiting can cover a wide range of gardens, though I suspect that the gimlet eye of those who inspect applicant gardens on behalf of the National Garden Scheme is a tad more inclined to favor the socially aspiring garden. That said, the determinedly traditional garden featured quite a bit when we used to do some Yellow Book tourism thirty years ago, especially where a group village opening offered half a dozen or so neighboring gardens ranging from the expansive affair attached to some Old Rectory that featured tasteful old roses, a white border, a clematis-hung pergola, a little pool with water lilies, flag irises and sisyrinchium, to the council-house garden with emphatic block plantings of annuals—calceolaria, red salvia, marigolds, a ribbon edging of white alyssum. This latter inclination seems to me to be the last gasp of Victorian carpet bedding, and actually is admirable in the sense that very probably all will have been grown from seeds—skillful gardening, in fact. But no longer either fashionable or classy. And if such a garden had a rose it would be one of the most flamboyant hybrid teas—"Peace"—or that hybrid tea/floribunda cross "Queen Elizabeth," both of them large, gaudy, and virtually indestructible.

Many plants are social indicators, and the rose is certainly that, hence the pointed references to roses in Angus Wilson's novel, striking a chord at once with the rose-sensitive reader. I was a relative rose innocent when we acquired the garden in Oxfordshire, and I realized at once that its previous owner had been both knowledgeable and fastidious. She had bequeathed us three big old shrub roses, two of which I never could identify, but one was "Rosa Mundi"—*Rosa gallica* "Versicolor"—and up the front of the house was the climber "Madame Alfred Carrière," both of these roses of choice for the connoisseur. We were off to a good start, and I winced a bit at the memory of the bed of "Iceberg" I had established in a previous garden—amiable hard-working white floribunda but somewhat unimaginative on my part.

It seems appropriate to consider the rose at some length: the one flower that everyone recognizes, the most ubiquitous of all garden plants, the most symbolic of flowers. Exquisite, wonderfully various, difficult. Christopher Lloyd, that celebrated gardener, staggered the gardening world when he junked his renowned rose garden at Great Dixter and created a tropical garden instead, calling roses "miserable and unsatisfactory shrubs." And gardeners may have been shocked, but will have taken the point. My grandmother had a large rose garden, sunken, very Jekyll/Lutyens in design, with an iris-fringed pool in the center, and much of her life was spent in the struggle against black spot: I can see her still, wearing that hessian apron with pocket stuffed with twine, secateurs, trowel, furiously spraying. The rose can be wayward, sulky, ungrateful, it bites back; I was out with my meager few this morning, dead-heading, and have a sore thumb now where "Evelyn" stabbed me. But . . . but it is also glorious, *sui generis*, ancient.

A rose appears on a Minoan fresco, 3,500 years old. Theophrastus was distinguishing cultivated from wild roses in the fourth century B.C. Pliny wrote of them, and there they are on those wonderful Pompeiian garden frescoes. The rose came into the garden from the wild; there are around 150 species of wild rose, native only to the northern hemisphere, and particularly favoring China—hence the arrival in the West of what were called China roses in the eighteenth century. Rose breeders have been tampering with the rose for centuries: the roses we have today are the result of tampering on a historic and majestic scale—hybridization, to be correct—a process that has given us the extraordinary range and variety that have been available for many years now, all descended from the three groups of Gallicas, Damasks and Albas. Jennifer Potter's magisterial work *The Rose* describes this process with an eloquence that is almost biblical: "the first Chinas mated with the European Gallicas and Damasks to beget the Bourbons, which then crossed and recrossed with the Portlands, the Chinas and the hybrid Chinas to produce the Hybrid Perpetuals; and the China Teas came together with the Hybrid Perpetuals to beget the Hybrid Teas, which then crossed on the one hand with the Dwarf Polyanthas or Polyantha Pompoms to beget the Hybrid Polyanthas . . ." I love this—fascinating, the determined pursuit of an ever-more perfect rose, a new variety, a more delicate scent, a more elegant fusion of reds and pinks and yellows and creams and whites and all the shades between and beyond. A new growth habit, a more tenacious resistance to disease. And it goes on still. David Austin's celebrated English Roses have introduced 190 new rose cultivars, making around 150,000 crosses a year, resulting in a quarter of a million seedlings which, at the end of a nine-year cycle, will give the breeder three or more new roses a year. It was his "Evelyn" that stabbed me just now; well worth it, she is superb—pink/apricot/peach, with an intoxicating scent.

Beyond the actual rose there is the symbolic rose, the flower that seems to have harvested more symbolism than any other. A symbol of silence, discretion, for the Romans, who had dining-room ceilings painted with roses so that guests were reminded that what was spoken in drink was "*sub rosa*" only, a custom that was revived in the seventeenth century. It is the emblem of that peculiar Protestant sect of the same period, the Rosicrucians, who held mystical beliefs apparently related to alchemy, with, it seems, descendent secret societies still around today. Their symbol had the rose fused with the Christian cross—the flower that also symbolized eternal love modifying the symbol of sacrifice. The association with love and sexuality goes back to the Greeks—the rose sacred to Aphrodite, goddess of love— and persists thereafter, and today, with all those red roses that fill the supermarkets for Valentine's Day. A Georgia O'Keeffe rose painting is a manifestation of the rose as image of female sexuality, though the artist dislikes this interpretation.

Religion, eroticism, and then the rose gets political, with the white rose of York and the red rose of Lancaster—a symbol of war, indeed, the Wars of the Roses. Taken over entirely by the Tudors, it becomes their emblem, that stylized, instantly recognizable rose—hijacked as a dynastic, political emblem.

Plenty of medicinal applications, from earliest times, used as an oil or rosewater as remedy at one time or another for just about everything from a headache onward. In a later age, it has declined to becoming simply the basis for pot-pourri (dried rose petals placed in bowls around the house for their scent), which I remember making once in indus-trial quantities, and then discovering that you end up with a lot of brown petals that don't smell of much for long. However, it seems that in 2008 a breakthrough in medical research was suggesting that a form of rose-hip powder might be effective in the treatment of arthritis. I read of this with interest, and wait to have it offered on the NHS.

And the dried rose petal has an urgent contemporary use. Forget potpourri—rose petals are confetti now. Environ-mentally undesirable paper confetti is banned by churches; the substitute is dried rose-petal confetti—nicely biodegrad-able. We discovered this in the course of planning for my granddaughter Rachel's wedding this year—and that there is an entire small industry selling the stuff, various websites, all charging what seemed like inflated prices. Right, this we can do ourselves. Family and friends were exhorted to get out there and sacrifice their roses (dead won't do—they must be in full flower, or just about to go over). You spread the petals out, well spaced, on newspaper, somewhere warm and dry, and lo! After three or four days you have acceptable confetti.

Most gardeners develop a personal relationship with roses, planting the same ones again and again, in garden after gar-den; in my own, and in family gardens, "Buff Beauty" and "New Dawn" crop up time and again, along with "Gertrude Jekyll" and "Constance Spry." We always had a "Penelope"—of course. Actually, a good bushy hybrid musk shrub rose with creamy pink flowers. It seems to have been introduced by an

English cleric called Joseph Pemberton in 1924, but I can't find who was the Penelope in question. It is the ultimate honor to have a rose named after you. My present garden is far too small to accommodate "Penelope," and I miss it. A favorite rose can map human habitation: Jennifer Potter tells of how an early American rose called "Harison's Yellow" was taken west by the pioneers of the 1840s and 1850s, its descendants thus mapping the course of the immigrant trails across the country. This makes me think at once of the loquat, its presence in north London gardens indicating that Greek Cypriots once lived here.

In fact, North America has always been as passionate about roses as Europe. Eleanor Perényi writes knowledgeably about the complexities of hybridization, but also a touch irritably, pointing out that sometimes the eternal pursuit of yet another novelty, another variation, can produce monstrosity, in her view, citing "Ambassador," introduced in 1980, and "glistening apricot . . . This range, a clamoring chorus of Sunkist oranges and corals . . . look hideous planted with other, traditionally colored roses." I have just summoned up "Ambassador" on the Internet, and I quite agree. She is more charitable than I am about flamboyant "Peace," and considers it beautiful, stressing its "romantic" story—bred by the French rose grower Meilland before the war, who sent his few cuttings to America to save them, those consigned to the American grower Robert Pyke being on the last plane to leave France in November 1940, before the German invasion. That rose was cultivated in America, and launched in 1945, with its iconic name. It is said to be the world's favorite rose, so I am quite out of step. But when Perényi writes of roses growing in the eastern United

States, and the need to "smother bushes in salt hay and wrap standards like mummies or bury them alive," I am startled. Roses not hardy! Needing winter protection! We forget how well off we gardeners are in this country's temperate climate—conditions that might have been designed for gardening.

This digression into the matter of the rose was prompted by its occasional role as social indicator. More generally, it is simply present in most gardens as the archetypal flower, the essential garden plant. I suppose you could say that possession of a garden is itself a social indicator, though that wouldn't be quite true—central London mansion apartments worth millions don't have gardens. But a government report of 2009 reckoned that by the following year 2.16 million homes would be without a private garden. It was expected that by 2020 just 89 percent of households were likely to have a garden (actually, I'm surprised it is that many), and this decline was blamed on the increased building of apartments by developers, and the easy permission to build on gardens, designated as "brownfield" land. In London two-thirds of front gardens are paved or concreted over. I remember that back when I was writing for children, in the 1980s, politically correct children's book editors reminded authors sternly that a garden is not an appropriate feature in a children's book, on the grounds that most—or many—children don't have one, forgetting that we read to escape and expand our circumstances, not to replicate them. I suppose that *Tom's Midnight Garden* would have been suspect.

At the other end of the spectrum stands the gardener, very much a social indicator in the past and indeed today. If you employ garden help, even on a very minor scale, you are displaying a degree of affluence. And in the archetypal Victorian or Edwardian garden, the gardener is an essential feature. Think of Mr. McGregor in *The Tale of Peter Rabbit*: the ominous "scr-r-ritch, scratch, scratch, scritch" of his hoe, after reading of which the sound of a hoe is forever loaded. Mr. McGregor wages war on rabbits; Peter Rabbit and his cousin Benjamin Bunny very nearly fall victim to him; Peter's father had been put in a pie by Mr. McGregor.

Now there is an ambiguity, in Beatrix Potter's work, as to whether Mr. McGregor's garden, as portrayed, is his own or whether he is employed therein. It seems to me that the garden is much too extensive to be a cottage garden: it is clearly a large walled and hedged kitchen garden, with a substantial greenhouse, frames and tubs, and in *The Tale of the Flopsy Bunnies*, which continues the engagement between McGregor and the rabbits unto the second generation, there is an illustration depicting the garden path and pergola arch of a considerable flower garden. Mr. McGregor's house is said to adjoin the garden; very likely, if the gardener's cottage. So I like to see Mr. McGregor as the archetypal gardener in literary fiction. When we were serious vegetable growers, and suffered rabbit intrusion, Jack used to say that he considered Mr. McGregor to be a much misunderstood man.

Furthermore, Mr. McGregor is presumably Scottish. There seems to have been a tradition since the eighteenth century that the significant gardener was a Scot—three of the seven founders of the Horticultural Society in 1804 were that. George Eliot wrote in *Adam Bede*, "a gardener is

Scottish as a French teacher is Parisian." So Mr. McGregor fits nicely.

P. G. Wodehouse tuned in to this tradition in *Blandings Castle*, where his Angus McAllister has to be the archetypal Scottish head gardener. We first meet him as seen by his employer, Lord Emsworth ("a fluffy-minded and amiable old gentleman")—"bent with dour Scottish determination to pluck a slug from its reverie beneath a leaf of lettuce." The relationship between the two of them is traditionally embattled. Permission from McAllister is required before any flower can be picked from the gardens: "They were bright with Achillea, Bignonia Radicans, Campanula, Digitalis, Euphorbia, Funkia, Gypsophila, Helianthus, Iris, Liatris, Monarda, Phlox Drummondi, Salvia, Thalictrum, Vinca, and Yucca. But the devil of it was that Angus McAllister would have a fit if they were picked. Across the threshold of this Eden the ginger whiskers of Angus McAllister lay like a flaming sword." He wants to create a gravel path through the Castle's famous yew alley, an idea that appalls Lord Emsworth, who is constantly on the back foot over this issue: "... he was wondering why Providence, if obliged to make head-gardeners, had found it necessary to make them so Scotch." The trouble is, he needs McAllister, who is the only person with the skill to cultivate a pumpkin of unbeatable quality that will win Lord Emsworth first prize for pumpkins at the Shrewsbury Show. He had once dismissed McAllister, the issue at that point being McAllister's refusal to send away a visiting American girl cousin of his to whom Lord Emsworth's renegade son Freddie has taken a fancy. McAllister refuses—"He made Scotch noises at the back of his throat"—and is sacked, but Lord Emsworth is eventually obliged to implore him to return, in the interests of the pumpkin. The relationship is beautifully presented, and you want more of McAllister, who is unfortunately only a flickering presence in the usual helter-skelter Wodehouse narrative. I found myself interested in that plant list, too; did Wodehouse know them all, or did he get them out of a catalog? Some had me stumped: liatris is a sort of purple bottle-brush, it seems—looks horrible—funkia is another name for hosta, *Bignonia radicans*—trumpet vine—was new to me. And that, along with several others, just doesn't sound like a promising cut flower. I suspect a dive into a catalog by a writer who wasn't himself an applied gardener.

My Egyptian childhood was richly populated with gardeners; my mother's extensive English-style garden required much upkeep. There was Mansour, the head gardener, of whom I was wary, because he was rightly suspicious of some of my activities, which might involve snapping off those intriguing yellow stamens in arum lilies, and would report on me. There was Ali, who was robust, jolly, and in charge of heavy duties like lawn mowing. And the garden boy, Ahmed, who swept paths, was around my age, and up for games like competitive hopping until chivvied back to work by an irate Mansour.

In the Oxfordshire garden with two streams we had help, but I can't think of Richard Taylor as our gardener: friend, collaborator. He and Jack would work together, in unceasing conversation; I would come out and find them paused, each leaning on spade or fork, when Jack had challenged

Richard's countryman's natural conservatism with some radical social or political proposition: "Now, Jack, I'm not sure I'm eye to eye with you there." Richard loved machinery, and his greatest joy was to find some appliance that didn't work, and bring it back to life. Jack would be alongside, like the plumber's mate, or the aide in an operating theater: "The spanner, Jack, please. Now can I have the small screwdriver, and the oilcan." Needless to say, he was a connoisseur of lawnmowers, and egged Jack on to acquire a stable of them; the Mountfield for the lawn, a ride-on thing for the paddock, and a fearful implement called the Bushwhacker for any more demanding operation; you could have cleared virgin forest with it. "I think we'll be needing the Bushwhacker for this job, Jack"; and off they'd go, eyes glinting. Most of all, Richard liked some new endeavor: "I've been thinking, what would you say to a stone arch between the bridge over the stream and the vegetable garden—there could be a rose over it?" The arch was built, expertly, by him; the rose, "New Dawn." I hope both are still there.

> Our England is a garden, and such gardens are not made
> By singing:—"Oh, how beautiful," and sitting in the shade.
> While better men than we go out and start their working
>   lives
> At grubbing weeds from gravel-paths with broken
>   dinner-knives.

The other garden poem that everyone knows, and in fact a poem about gardeners; it is clear that the sort of garden

Kipling has in mind is distinctly upper class, and a garden dependent on the gardener, on gardeners:

> For where the old thick laurels grow, along the thin
>   red wall,
> You'll find the tool- and potting-sheds which are the heart
>   of all.
> The cold-frames and the hot-houses, the dung-pits and
>   the tanks,
> The rollers, carts, and drain-pipes, with the barrows and
>   the planks.
>
> And there you'll see the gardeners, the men and
>   'prentice boys
> Told off to do as they are bid and do it without noise;
> For, except when seeds are planted and we shout to scare
>   the birds,
> The Glory of the Garden it abideth not in words.

This is the classic Victorian and Edwardian garden with all the accessories, the hired labor being the most critical of all. Kipling and his wife, Carrie, created a garden at Bateman's, in Sussex, the seventeenth-century house in which the family lived for over thirty years, and which Carrie left to the National Trust. So he was certainly into garden design—an alley with a pergola covered in pears, a walled kitchen garden converted from a stable yard, discrete areas within yew hedges—but you wonder if he did any of that grubbing up with a broken dinner-knife himself. I doubt it; though the reference is perceptive, and accurate—that is indeed a useful gardening implement (unless—perish the thought—the term is there simply for the rhyme). Those thirty-three acres of garden, meadows and woods would have been worked by others, in the early twentieth century—that traditional army of gardeners.

Hestercombe, near Taunton, is a medieval house substantially made over in the seventeenth century, and distinguished now for its gardens, run by the Hestercombe Gardens Trust. The gardens are one of the finest Lutyens/ Jekyll collaborations. They were commissioned by the then owners of the house, Viscount Portman and his wife, and the gardens laid out between 1904 and 1906. They are splendid—very Lutyens, very Jekyll, with flights of stone steps, parterre with Jekyll planting, rills with pools, woodland walks and lakes beyond. But what, for me, evokes that earlier, Edwardian life of this garden—any grand garden, perhaps—is the group portrayed on a postcard you can find in Hestercombe's shop.

These are the gardeners, posed for a formal portrait— seventeen of them, one row seated, one row standing, and flanked at one side by a lad of maybe twelve, and at the other by a white-bearded figure in his seventies. All wear hats—flat caps for the most part. Shirt and waistcoat seem to be *de rigueur*; all but one of the seven seated figures at the front wear aprons. Those standing behind are posed with hoe, spade, rake, shears, while the sitters are neatly framed by two long-spouted watering-cans. They inspire confidence, these gardeners; formally dressed, business-like. You feel that Hestercombe would have been well serviced. One of them must be the head gardener, a figure of authority,

and who would have had considerable horticultural expertise. Scottish?

A garden of that order will not be serviced by seventeen
men today. But one must remember that garden work, just
like housework, has been turned on its head by modern
appliances: the strimmer, the electric hedge-cutter, the
rotovator. Hestercombe might have had one of the early
petrol-driven lawnmowers, but that was a paltry affair compared with today's powerful products. Half of those
seventeen Edwardian gardeners could probably be dis-
pensed with by reason of technological advance; and,
indeed, I learn that in 2016 Hestercombe employs just six
gardeners; three with horticultural training and three
trained in countryside management.

Today's gardener is much more likely to be seen as a
professional—graduate of a horticultural college like Capel
Manor in London, and elsewhere. And television—the
Chelsea and Hampton Court flower shows, *Gardeners'
World*, and other television gardening programs—have
promoted the concept of the gardener as celebrity, all those
celebrity presenters, clearly knowledgeable, clearly professional, all those designer gardeners with their show garden
that you either covet or loathe but know that either way you
are never going to rise (or sink) to anything like that. These
people are a far cry from the lowly gardening laborer of
the nineteenth and early twentieth centuries, though of
course these are still there but likely now to be interns,
apprentices with an eye to a future in the profession. Every
week, another card drops through my door alerting me to
the arrival of a new garden services firm—maintenance,

landscaping, any work undertaken. These will have been set up and are managed by someone with plenty of horticultural qualifications and—in my experience—the labor force is likely to be Czech, Polish, Bulgarian, possessed of rather fewer of those, if any. I always need a firm to do the autumn clearing-up work, and high-pressure hosing of the paving, and am still grumpy about my experience of Czech Tom, who hacked my *Hydrangea petiolaris* right back, evidently ignorant of the fact that it flowers on the new growth. But I have had excellent experiences as well, and one has to admire the versatility; Polish Marek, here for a morning, was really an engineer, he told me, marking time until he found more appropriate work, but he efficiently cleared away the intrusive polygonum from over the wall without molesting the hydrangea.

This topic of the gardener seemed relevant to a discussion of the garden as social indicator, but what is clear is that the status and persona of the gardener has changed radically over time. The grubber-up of weeds from gravel paths has given way to, at one end of the spectrum, the television personality, and, at the other, most likely, the employee of a small business. A bit different in the country, where the jobbing gardener is still around. Nevertheless, to be a user of garden services of any kind implies a certain affluence; the serviced garden puts its owner in one category rather than another. The other being, as always, most gardens up and down the land where the only service is likely to be a press-ganged child, or that useful neighbor who happens to own a strimmer.

Interestingly, gardening as an activity has not been seen as socially demeaning. The upper-class lady has always got her hands dirty—look at Vita Sackville-West, let alone Gertrude Jekyll and her many followers. My grandmother—solidly middle rather than upper—gardened for several hours every day of her life, but she was aghast when obliged occasionally to do the washing up, in the post-war years of domestic labor scarcity, while to scrub a floor or operate a vacuum cleaner would have been out of the question. Gardening was one thing, housework quite another. For Elizabeth von Arnim, of course, Prussian etiquette in the early twentieth century forbade her from getting stuck in with a trowel—evidently perceptions were different over there. But when I doubted if Kipling himself ever grubbed out weeds it was because he had the labor force, and would have seen himself as more usefully occupied at his desk; nobody would have raised an eyebrow if he had chosen to do a bit of recreational gardening. It does seem odd now, this early-twentieth-century view that social status made one kind of physical activity—work, you could call it—acceptable and another very much not. Gardening, you get a lot hotter and dirtier than you do dusting a room or washing a floor. But gardening was a genteel occupation, housework a demeaning task that you paid someone else to do. I can understand to the extent that I enjoy gardening and don't particularly relish housework, but my grandmother's view, and that of her generation and beyond, wasn't much to do with the pleasure factor, it was an entrenched position: gardening was constructive, requiring skill and knowledge, whereas you never involved yourself with housework because that could perfectly well be done by others, and always had been.

My grandmother, like most women of her kind and her

time, couldn't cook. A minor aspect of the social revolution of the last hundred years is that today all middle-class women can cook, most of them with great competence. All cook, while probably rather fewer garden with enthusiasm. Cooking could be said to have usurped the role of gardening, for the middle class; a person who is a good cook (men can step forward here too) is respected for being so, cookery skill is seen as admirable. Again, television probably has had an effect on this attitude, affording more airtime by far to cookery than to gardening programs, but the change seems to me to do also with enhanced expectations about food, deriving from foreign travel, and a perception that to cook well needs skill and application. And to the fact that a paid cook is no longer affordable for the vast majority.

So, among the various social reversals of the last century is that that has made competence at cookery a desirable attribute. And while gardening was always seen as a genteel activity, the garden is perhaps now regarded as an extension of the house, a property asset that should be kept in good order. What kind of order will depend on the inclination of the owner, on gardening style. And style is of course a broad church, with ankle-deep grass, washing line and child's rusting tricycle at one extreme, and at the other the Chelsea-inspired curving paths, water feature with fountain, patio and pergola, fastidious planting. Some of us garden, some are gardened, others get out there once a year with that borrowed strimmer.

Foreign travel has affected our approach to food, in this country, but I am doubtful as to whether the same thing can be said about gardening. I am going to get xenophobic here: we garden rather well. I am tempted to say we garden second to none. There have been, there are, many notable, unrivaled, individual gardeners—designers, writers—from elsewhere, but in a general, homely, back (and front) garden way I think that we Brits do a pretty good job. We have our grand gardens, the landscaped gardens inspired by the eighteenth-century picturesque taste that identify English gardening: every language has the term, it seems—*jardin à l'anglaise, giardino all'inglese, Englischer Landschaftsgarten.* This is Rousham, Stowe, Stourhead—your lakes, bridges, temples. That bold new concept of garden landscaping is entirely English. But that is not really what I am thinking of. Most of us do not have a landscape to garden—we manipulate a few square yards, or rather more if you are lucky. But there is still something essentially English about that manipulation. And what is that? What swims before the eyes when you think of an English garden? Grass, most definitely—the lawn, from the rolling expanse to the carefully tended back-garden pocket handkerchief. Paths—our gardens offer journeys, long or short, paved, graveled. Water—we love a pond, anything from the generous lake with willows and carpet of water lilies to the membrane-lined hole in the ground, now teeming with tadpoles and water boatmen. But, above all, texture, color and informality. English gardens do not wear a straitjacket; they are lush, exuberant, expansive. Richly planted—the old concept of the herbaceous border. We like size and emphasis—where would we be without the hydrangea, the buddleia, the shrub rose? Roses, roses, all the way. Roses up, as well as roses down—up the house, up the walls. We garden in every dimension, subsume our houses into our gardens. The English garden is about color, variety—the exploitation of seasonal change, the continuity whereby spring segues into summer, summer dies away into autumn—and about the iconic plants without which we could not do: the rose, the rose, and clematis, fuchsias, lavender, pansies, narcissi, tulips, peonies, irises—all these and more. How they fit together is where the lack of the straitjacket comes in, the element of careless abandon, not untidiness but a knack of siting this where it would complement that, creativity with shapes and colors, not so much design as a shrewd approach to plants and what can be done with them.

Elsewhere, when it comes to gardening, there is of course French style—Le Nôtre and all that geometry, straight lines in every direction—or the Italian Renaissance gardens with their terraces and fountains. Distinctive enough but of their time; I do not think there are other gardening styles current today that are as immediately identifiable as our own is. Japanese, perhaps, with their addiction to rocks and swept gravel, but this impression comes from images of show gardens; do ordinary Japanese gardeners do that sort of thing in their backyards? I am short on evidence here, but it does seem to me that the English garden stands alone when it comes to that quality of being instantly known.

We have an immediate advantage: the climate. The temperate climate that means plenty of rain for those lawns, and for everything else, few prolonged extremes of either cold or heat, a long growing period. If you can't manage to garden competently with those benedictions you are a pretty duff gardener. A clever gardener can garden anywhere: Mediterranean gardens with that judicious choice of drought-resistant plants. But you don't have to be particularly clever in this country—just ancestrally attuned to a certain style that is about grass, and lavish, imaginatively informal planting.

So . . . From social style to national style. And it is social style that is the more pertinent here, both for the way in which it crops up so aptly in fictional contexts, and the demonstration of it all around, if you do but look. There may be a quintessentially English garden style, but the interpretation of it depends on personal idiosyncrasy, and that in turn is a matter of who you are and, probably, how your parents and grandparents gardened. My personal theory that the urge to garden is genetic ties in with ancestral garden-style conditioning: if your mother and grandmother gardened, you are likely to do so as well, and the way in which you garden owes much to your social context. Patrician gardening is an acreage of pergolas and laburnum walks away from the council-house mixed border and vegetable plot, though today this gradation is complicated by the effect of gardening fashion, by the manipulation of garden centers and television gardening programs. We garden according to who we are, but also according to commercial enticement and media influence. The garden today is a perilous place, one in which we express our personal taste, which itself derives from our time and our circumstances. And that is what makes gardens so fascinatingly various, and so eloquent.

Town and Country

Those familiar with Beatrix Potter's *The Tale of Johnny Town-Mouse* will recall that it is the most succinct literary statement going of the apposition between town and country. Town life, as perceived by Timmy Willie, the country mouse who arrives in town by accident in the carrier's produce hamper, is alarming (cats, the cook armed with a poker), amoral (the town mice live by pilfering), pretentious ("the dinner was of eight courses, not much of anything, but truly elegant") and noisy (dogs bark, boys whistle, a canary sings like a steam engine). Country life is wholesome—Timmy Willie has been reared on roots and salad, rather than pilfered bacon—arcadian (the smell of violets and spring grass), organic (Timmy Willie makes herb pudding and shells corn and seeds from his autumn store), peaceful (the garden in which he lives has roses, pinks and pansies and no noise except birds and bees). Johnny Town-Mouse visits, is distressed by mud and cows, and returns to town in the next hamper, complaining of the quiet. I suspect that all those exposed to this seminal work in formative years are deeply indoctrinated. It is made quite clear where Miss Potter's preference lies, and the authorial voice is compelling—no sensitive four-year-old is going to do other than line up behind her. Country is good, town is bad; any right-minded person prefers to live in a country garden, eating seeds and sniffing the violets.

I'm inclined to agree, to some extent, having declined from an acre or so of lush Oxfordshire to a few square yards of London. But that is mere depreciation of resources; what is at issue in the Potter subtext is something much deeper—a moral status. I met that when newly arrived in England from Egypt in 1945, a bewildered twelve-year-old. I had town and country grandmothers, and was shuttled between them. There was no question of who held the upper hand—my Somerset granny with her vast garden and a skyful of fresh air. The Harley Street one could fight back with culturally instructive museum visits and Shakespeare in the Regent's Park Open Air Theatre, but must concede smog, smuts and traffic.

The apposition continues today, of course, and was perhaps epitomized by the demonstrations over the fox-hunting ban in 2004, when 400,000 country-clad cohorts of the Countryside Alliance filled Parliament Square. The law that was passed was a masterly compromise that left hunting both banned and not banned, so that it went on in some form anyway. But the fuss must have baffled much of the urban population largely unaware of fox hunting in any case and with no strong views, except for those suffering from fox depredation of refuse sacks and gardens, who would have seen organized fox control as an excellent idea. The legislation was all about Tony Blair's need as prime minister to mollify a section of his party, but nevertheless it brought about a nice statement of the divide between town and country. Part of the nation, it seemed, lived in the country and spent its time chasing and slaughtering animals, and the other part hadn't known much about this but, when enlightened, felt vague righteous disapproval.

I am concerned specifically with gardens, but the wider issue of rural-versus-urban is relevant. The two-million-plus gardenless households are more likely to be urban than rural; it was ever thus, at least since towns and cities became more densely populated. For country people, a garden is assumed, pretty well; in the city you may be blessed with your own patch, but quite likely not. The suburban garden is another matter entirely; more on that later.

It was in the early 1940s that town and country became most conscious of the divide. Those who took in evacuee children from London and elsewhere were made aware for the first time of the nature of urban poverty; the evacuee children, in turn, found a world they had not known existed, in which there were animals they had never seen, such as cows and sheep, and in which people had gardens. Some city children would indeed have had a back space of some kind, but it would have housed the coals, and in many cases an outdoor toilet. The country garden was an eye-opener. My grandmother had Stepney evacuees under the age of six throughout the war; her house was a classified war nursery. One five-year-old boy discovered the Cedar of Lebanon on the lawn within a day or two of arrival, shinned gleefully up it, and had to be recovered by the local fire brigade.

Town and country gardens are differently composed, as I know well, having gardened both. The country garden consists of soil, acid or alkaline according to region, nicely populated with worms, perhaps with some intriguing garden archaeology by way of broken clay pipes, fragments of pretty blue-and-white china, the occasional little old bone spoon or tiny glass medicine bottle (thus, my Oxfordshire garden). The city garden has bricks, cat shit, lengths of rusty barbed wire, nails, lumps of coke and crisp packets, all encased in perfunctory black earth that the worms have long since abandoned in disgust. I felt instant empathy when reading Karel Čapek's account of his Czech town garden. The archaeology is more disconcerting than intriguing: the occasional bundle of plastic that you prefer not to investigate. My present London garden wasn't quite as dismaying as this, and we addressed its deficiencies at once with paving, raised beds and an onslaught of topsoil and chicken manure, but the first one certainly was. Our next-door neighbor there had dug up the carcass of a London taxi in his, complete with seating and steering wheel.

There is a stark apposition between town and country garden marauders. In the town, it is foxes and other people's cats. In the country, a fine range of wildlife: rabbits, moles, badgers, pigeons, pheasants. The country fox has better things to do. In the Somerset garden, we have had hare incursion—three leverets found under a lavender bush, presumably the progeny of an inexperienced mother not aware that hares are supposed to park their offspring in a field. The town gardener can wage war on foxes and cats, up to a point; the country gardener is on the back foot, unless sufficiently cold-blooded to resort to mole traps and a shotgun. My own view, country gardening, was that the wildlife was there first, as it were, and can be said to have certain rights of occupation; the gardener is the incomer and must expect to pay a price. Except for pheasants, which are not native, are going to be shot anyway and should keep to their target areas and leave the hellebore buds alone.

City gardening is not for the faint-hearted, but the committed urban gardener will achieve wonders: I have seen more imaginative and resourceful gardens in London than anywhere else. Moreover, there is that urge, on the part of some, to make something out of the most unpromising circumstances. I live in a part of London awash with early-nineteenth-century terrace houses. So, houses with a basement and an area (possibly mine is the last generation to know that the sunken space outside the basement window, between that and the pavement wall, is called the area; I have had young builders look at me in bewilderment when I asked them to bring things in by way of the area, and they weren't Polish builders either). The basements round here are often separate apartments, and I think it is most likely to be the apartment-dwellers who create an unexpected little sanctuary below ground level. You look down, and discover a blaze of geraniums, a *Trachelospermum jasminoides* covering a carefully constructed trellis, a clematis, tree ferns, bamboo, an array of cacti; a place, often, in which every inch has been made use of for a pot of something or a tray of something else, all thriving away in the microclimate down there. Since I have the garden, my own area is rather under-exploited, but I make sure that there is always a pot or two of ferns, and that the iron trough basket fixed to the wall is planted up with diascia for the summer, and bulbs for the spring—"Tête-à-Tête" daffodils, or I shall try "Elka" for next year, which sounds like a satisfactorily miniature daff for that position. Oh, the annual treat of poring over the Avon Bulbs catalog, trying to decide between one alluring offering and another. Shall I have "Purissima," or

"Calgary Flames"? Plant names are a minefield. Those who name can be disastrously overinventive. Tulips seem to have been named with relative restraint; a rush of poetic description is acceptable—"Apricot Beauty," "Grand Perfection." But as a fuchsia lover I wince at the unfortunate trio named "Shrimp Cocktail," "Pink Fizz" and "Icing Sugar," let alone the equally put-upon dahlia called "Badger Twinkle." David Austin's determinedly prosaic naming of my ground-cover roses is preferable: "Hertfordshire," "Cambridgeshire," "Worcestershire."

Gardeners are a community—there should be some sort of Masonic handshake. As it is, when you sniff out a fellow gardener there is instant communion, and I particularly like the presence of these invisible, unknown, surrounding neighbors, who have seized the day in the sense of exploiting the unpromising. Two or three square yards of concrete, six feet below the pavement, and you can create a personal display.

Perhaps the gardening urge is innate, present in most of us as a legacy of humanity's move from hunter-gathering into settling down and growing stuff to live off. The throwback hunter-gatherer part of us sends us off to the supermarket; the innovative streak drives us outside to dig and plant. Not an explanation to press too far, but it would put a certain kind of gardener firmly into the Neolithic revolution category, as the archaeologists like to call it: the vegetable gardener, above all the allotment gardener.

I have never had an allotment, but I have grown vegetables in a double-allotment-size kitchen garden, so I can feel a certain empathy with the committed allotmenteer. I know what it is to be digging the potato trench, planting out the onion sets, nipping the tops off broad beans before the blackfly get there, cursing carrot fly, harvesting courgettes before they turn into truncheons. The vegetable gardener is an embattled figure (Mr. McGregor, again . . .) and vegetable growing is hard work. But many people want to do it. There are long waiting lists for allotments, countrywide. In London, you can wait years.

The history of the allotment movement goes back to the early eighteenth century, but today's allotmenteer can be rather different from those for whom the original allotments were designed, the rural poor—and, later, the urban poor too. Valentine Low has written of contemporary London allotment life in his book *One Man and His Dig*, which contrives to be both entertaining and nicely informative, and describes his own allotment site in west London as providing allotments for an Afghan, a Pole, Moroccans, West Indians, a Goan, Irish, and "*Guardian*-reading middle-class types." The adjoining main site could boast Iraqis, Portuguese, Italian, Libyan and Spanish. The twenty-first-century allotmenteer is quite likely to be middle class or from an ethnic minority. And while these last may well be not at all well off, the allotment population, at least in London, would seem to be a far cry from the laboring poor for whom the allotment movement was devised.

The creation of the original allotment spaces in the eighteenth and nineteenth centuries was intended as a way to alleviate poverty and also to stem the mass exodus from the countryside by rural laborers on subsistence wages hoping for a better life in the cities. By 1890 there were 445,000 allotments across the country, and laws were passed obliging local councils to provide allotments if there was a demand. By then, the demand came just as much in urban areas—the tradition of the town allotment was under way. And then came the First World War, which sent the demand for allotments into overdrive, both on the part of those who wanted one, and the government, desperate to increase the supply of home-grown food. Every spare bit of land must be turned into growing space; free gardening advisory pamphlets were distributed. By 1917 a further 12,000 acres had been turned into allotments, but even so, the supply never kept up with the demand, though by the end of the war there was one allotment to every five households, providing eight to ten million people with food. Parks and playing fields were turned into allotments; in South Wales miners were provided with allotments by the collieries.

Indeed, it could be said that the concept of the allotment as both a right for all and a distinct need for many was set firm in the First World War. The demand for allotments continued after the war, but there was a huge need now for land for housing, at the expense of the provision of allotments. Allotmenteers organized themselves into the National Union of Allotment Holders, and pressured government into passing the 1922 Allotment Act, giving allotment holders better security and requiring councils to provide allotments under given circumstances. Later acts defined statutory allotment sites and made allotments a part of every town-planning scheme. The allotment site was now pretty well entrenched as a part of the landscape, and then received a tremendous boost with the outbreak of war in 1939.

Dig for Victory. The cheery posters and the vigorous exhortations were prompted by a very real potential crisis: food imports were drastically curtailed because all shipping space was needed for war supplies. Before the war, Britain had imported two-thirds of its food needs; in December 1939 it was considered that food supplies could last for another three months. If there were not to be disastrous shortages, or starvation, the country was going to have to provide for itself.

And it did, more or less. The objective was another 500,000 allotments, mainly in urban areas, and the pre-war total of 740,000 leaped to 1.75 million by the end of 1943. An immense swathe of potatoes and cabbages and peas and beans and onions and leeks up and down the land, and, indeed, rabbits and chickens as well—they were lumped in with vegetables. The families thus provided would have eaten well, compared with the rest of the population. And they would have been a small minority; their surplus—you always have a surplus, in some areas, as a vegetable grower: a runner bean mountain, or the lettuces gone mad—must have made them highly desirable friends or neighbors. Much land was requisitioned for allotment use—parks and playing fields, again—and by March 1944 domestic agriculture accounted for 10 percent of all food produced in Britain. That means a generation who learned to garden in the 1940s, for whom the activity had become a necessity, and saw to it that there would always, in some quarters, be a demand for a few rods of land and the freedom to grow whatever you wanted in it.

The demand has continued: witness the lengthy allotment waiting lists today. I suspect that were I forty years younger and living where I am now with just my small paved back garden I would have my name on my local council's waiting list. As it is, I am still nostalgic for the satisfactions of vegetable growing—that plunge of the fork to turn up the first new potatoes, getting a pick of French beans for supper, riffling through the seed catalogs for something new and interesting. Vegetable variety is endlessly fascinating, not least the naming thereof, and it was ever thus; a 1920 pamphlet called "The Allotment," I discover, had eighteen kinds of potato, including "Sharpe's Express," "British Queen," "Great Scot" and "King Edward VII" (would the king have felt entirely honored to have a potato named after him? A rose is another matter), six kinds of onion, various carrots including one called "Red Elephant."

Furthermore, judging by the forensic account given by Valentine Low in his book, I would have found allotment life something of a revelation. He describes the camaraderie, the sense of community, the tendency for people to help each other out, with advice or equipment. Where this last is concerned, he is specific about allotment etiquette when, on one occasion, he considers buying a strimmer, and realizes that that "just wasn't very allotment. People on allotments solve their problems with old bits of junk, with tools they have been using for decades or—if they are absolutely forced to spend money—with equipment they have bought from the Poundstretcher for an absolute pittance . . . It is not so much penny-pinching as thriftiness . . . how much more satisfying it is to solve your problems with a bit of artful make-and-mend than by just driving off to B&Q and waving your credit card around the place." Accordingly, carpet off-cuts are acquired from an Allied Carpets skip to cover a compost heap, sheds are built from old doors and lengths of salvaged wood, fences made from discarded central heating pipes and nylon string, corrugated plastic becomes a polytunnel and an old pram is revived as a wheelbarrow. I like this—the lateral thinking, the talent for innovation—and it explains that always arresting impression of individuality you get when your train slows down as it passes an allotment site, and you glimpse dozens of plots doing dozens of different things, and those architecturally challenged little shacks with a folding chair outside. Low is illuminating on allotment culture of today, and, having investigated the history of his own site, the change from the relative formality of dress fifty years ago ("I think that if I wore a tie to the allotment someone would have me sectioned"), and in social composition from the entirely white population of the allotments back then to the multicultural group of the twenty-first century. He is intrigued by this taste for gardening among immigrants, and wonders if it may have something to do with an ancestral memory, for many, of what their parents and grandparents did, even if they have never before got their hands into the soil themselves.

Paul Farley and Michael Symmons Roberts, in their book *Edgelands*, eloquently site allotments in their subject area: "Allotments signal that you are now passing through the edgelands as emphatically as a sewage works or a power station. They thrive on the fringes, the in-between spaces; on land left over (or left behind) by the tides of building and industrial development, in pockets behind houses or factories, and in ribbons along the trackbeds of railways." And, indeed, for someone like me, who has never actually worked one, they are inevitably associated with train journeys, that moment of looking out of the window and realizing that this is an edge-lands, as the allotments appear, a world of their own, a different, defiant place, both personal and collective. "They flaunt their functionality; the domestic garden with its hands dirty, busy and raddled with agriculture's businesslike clutter. They don't fit in. Minutes after leaving a central station, and the privatized shiny surfaces of the city, and there they lie, a cobbling together, like a refugee camp for those fleeing consumerism." Apparently, after a major report in the 1960s on their use and future, allotments might have been renamed "leisure gardens." What an appalling idea—not that it would ever have caught on. The allotment is not a garden; it is somehow more serious than that. And while I may never have worked an allotment I know very well that vegetable gardening has nothing to do with leisure: it is hard, blistering work. The authors of that report must have missed the point entirely, failing to see that the desire, the need, to work an allotment is something more atavistic than gardening itself, and certainly unrelated to any concept of leisure.

This discussion of the allotment has somehow fallen into a section about town and country; in fact, the allotment belongs properly to neither, a signal occupant of the Farley–Symmons Edgelands, slung between urban and rural as significantly as landfill tips, wastelands, industrial estates. They are tacked on to the town or city, depend on urban servicing, but have also a determined rural flavor, *sui generis*, a place of their own.

The great, the ubiquitous margin between town and country is of course suburbia. Eight out of ten people in England live in the suburbs; the suburban house has a garden, which accounts for a hefty percentage of consumers who may have some interest in garden-related products. Hence, presumably, the rise and rise of the garden center. But interest will vary from intense commitment to total absence thereof. The other intriguing train-window study is that slide show of suburban gardens that back on to a railway line: a spectrum of garden practice from assiduous cultivation—shaven lawn, flower beds, fruit trees, a vegetable plot—to careless abandon, with shaggy grass and assorted detritus. And the suburban garden is itself a blanket term, covering another spectrum, in which those slivers of gardens seen from the train are at one end, and at the other the substantial leafy parkland, by comparison, attached to more prosperous suburbias up and down the country; the plump commuter homes in tree-lined roads, each with its own dollop of land behind. Occasionally, some television program gives you an aerial view of such a landscape and you realize what an acreage of green there is (4 percent of land area in the United Kingdom), not countryside, not rural, but gardenside, and a considerable area, accounting for the Royal Society for the Protection of Birds' assertion that suburban gardens are essential to the survival of some bird populations. Half of all garden owners feed the birds on their site, it seems; that's a serious amount of peanuts and mixed seeds. Plenty of the gardens will be patrolled by a domestic cat, but apparently there is no scientific evidence that cat predation has a significant effect on bird populations. So the suburban garden is not just a potential pleasure for its owner, but is an environmental asset.

"Suburban" is a pejorative term, I suppose, precisely because the suburbs are neither town nor country, an interface, not one thing or the other. Suburban suggests a sort of mediocrity, inferiority, which seems a misplaced patronage when you think of the extent and the variety of suburbia. A patronage which derives perhaps from the concept of Metroland, the name given to the areas north and west of London that were developed in the early twentieth century, served by the Metropolitan Railway—the swathes of Tudor-bethan semis, "stockbroker country," that came to invite either distaste or the Betjeman affection that is itself a form of patronage. All that half-timbering—but all those gardens, also, one thinks, and generous gardens, back then. Most of them still there, except where infill building has been allowed, and contributing to that great rash of greenery between the city and the country proper.

Having gardened both urban and rural, I fancy the idea of those gardens: not too large, not too small, the sort of space that lends itself to creative design—hence all those television makeover programs in which startled owners are confronted with a garden that has gone Mediterranean, or sub-tropical, or has been graveled, paved and prinked out of all recognition. I could do with that, I think, eyeing my skimpy urban patch. It was a splendid concept, the suburban garden, back in its beginnings, the assumption that every home should have its quota of land, the equivalent to those two acres and a cow, and accounting today for this national wealth of gardens. Cause for celebration, not patronage.

This consideration of town and country—apposition, contrast—takes me to some final thoughts about what gardens do to us, and what we have done with them. I have looked at the ways in which writers—and painters—use gardens, at the vicissitudes of garden fashion, at gardening as a social indicator, at the ways in which a garden defies time and order. Gardens are integral to the psyche, it seems to me; even if you are not yourself a gardener, you would be offended if some unimaginably perverse system of the future declared gardens a proscribed asset: there shall be no gardens. Our most central mythology tells us that we began in a garden—and were expelled from it by an authority that forbade the acquisition of knowledge (Eve's action has always seemed to me both natural and commendable). Maybe that has something to do with the universal regard for gardens, for the concept of the garden: the ideal space where you would like to be. Not necessarily in order to dig and plant (you can leave that to those addicted) but just to be at one with things growing, flowering, with the cycle of the year, with the natural world (in so far as a garden can be said to be natural).

So I like to think there is something primeval about our affinity with gardens; most people appreciate a garden, a few want to get in there digging or weeding or improving, others just want to sit in the shade singing, "Oh, how beautiful." Maybe we are harking back to the expulsion ("Here we are, in possession again . . ."); more plausibly, we just enjoy being out of doors in a particularly beguiling place, and we recognize the creativity that is latent in almost any garden. Someone has manipulated this space, enhanced it, tried to make it beautiful or productive.

We like gardens, we need gardens, whether private or

communal. The public garden, large or small, park or village green, has not been included in this discussion; I have been concerned with the personal aspect of gardens and gardening. But the public garden—the park—is the expressed recognition that available outdoor space is a requirement for all. Cities, towns, must have green spaces—look at any urban map and you will see them. London is speckled all over with green, from the great expanses of Hampstead Heath and Richmond Park through the smaller parks and commons to the many garden squares, that perfect architectural concept, on one of which I live. And as I look out at it today, on a cold, crisp, sunny winter afternoon, it is being made use of by two small boys kicking a ball around, someone airing a baby in a buggy, an elderly man, well wrapped up, reading his newspaper on a bench. Maybe the primeval need is just that: the urge to be outside. We are not bred to be perpetually under cover; our Paleolithic ancestors retreated to the cave at night, a refuge and a base. Whether hunter-gathering or the first farmers, we have been more out than in; we are prone to cabin fever and claustrophobia. Though the essential salutary benefit of "fresh air" is a relatively modern cult; in earlier centuries the average laborer wouldn't have seen it quite like that. It was certainly a twentieth-century phenomenon; my grandmother would bundle me outside, as a teenager, if spotted lurking indoors with a book on a fine day. And it was into the garden that I was bundled; that was what it was for.

Along with much else. We cultivate our gardens for different reasons—to pick it, to eat it, to keep up with the neighbors, to get into the pages of the Yellow Book and open up in aid of charity. But the prime reason, the significant reason, is because we want to—because we have the gardening instinct, we are part of the community of gardeners. I am that, and probably you are too, if you have stuck thus far with this book. Those of us that way inclined would be severely deprived without a garden.

When you find that you are a gardener, things change; this latent addiction does not take over your life—it can't, you have other commitments—but it gives it new direction. Not just in terms of spare-time employment, but you now have extra vision—gardening vision. All right, this may sound extravagant, but I think it is true; you see the world with gardening eyes, you see what is growing where, you appreciate and assess and you wonder what that is if it is unfamiliar, and furthermore your situation in time is subtly changed, part of you lives now in garden time; you project forward, and back, you are no longer stuck always in the here and now.

A murky January day, and the green nubs of bulbs are poking up all over the place when I go out into the garden: snowdrops, narcissi, even the early tulips. Aha! Spring is not just a calendar promise, it is fact. It will happen. And I have jumped ahead; in the mind's eye, I am anticipating all that color and variety, wondering if *Tulipa* "Prinses Irene" will be as handsome as the Avon Bulbs catalog suggested.

I am only the most amateur gardener, and have felt some temerity in writing a book about gardening. But I have written here not so much about gardening as about the effect that gardens and gardening have: their charisma. And to know a little about something is also to be able to recognize the depth and complexity of the subject; my own limited experience has fostered my admiration for the great gardeners, the garden writers, the botanists. I have learned from them, but most of all I have discovered the extent of gardening lore, its history, its infinite variety, the wonderful possibilities of growing what you want where you want. I have tried to explore that here, to look at gardens and gardening as directives, to focus on the impact that they have, on how gardening people behave, on how gardens affect us.

Personal experience comes into it—a personal experience that I suspect most gardening people will recognize. My own life in the garden has been a particular, and special, aspect of life in general: the activity, the preoccupation, to which I have retreated both in practice and in the mind when everything else permitted. Get out there and dig, weed, prune, plant, when stuck with whatever was being written. Escape winter by swinging forward into spring, summer: maybe try those climbing French beans this year, what about a new rose, divide the irises, the leucojums are crowded—put some under the quince tree. The gardening self becomes a separate persona, waiting to be indulged when possible, and never entirely subdued—always noticing, appreciating, recording. This will be the case for anyone with a consuming interest (I hate that term "hobby") but gardening has this embracing quality in that it colors the way you look at the world: everything that grows, and the way in which it grows, now catches your attention; the gardening eye assesses, queries, is sometimes judgmental— quite opinionated, gardeners. The physical world has a new eloquence.

Whether gardening a window box or a swathe of Gloucestershire, you have acquired a gardening persona, and the vision that goes with it. For me, life in the garden has been both formative and essential; it has given me gardener's eyes and an extra way of looking about me, and an abiding and enriching engagement, whether I have been out there and hands-on in the garden, or just gardening in the mind, planning for the future, conjuring up virtual gardens.

Index

Index

Index

Index